Short Indiana Road Trips

Tourism Guide for Short Indiana Day Trips

Exploring Indiana's Highways and Back Roads Series

Paul R. Wonning

Short Indiana Road Trips

Short Indiana Road Trips

Published By Paul R. Wonning

Copyright 2017 by Paul R. Wonning

Print Edition

All rights reserved.

mossyfeetbooks@gmail.com

If you would like email notification of when new Mossy Feet books become available email the author for inclusion in the subscription list.

Mossy Feet Books

www.mossyfeetbooks.com

Indiana Places

http://indianaplaces.blogspot.com/

Description

Embark on a voyage of discovery with this travel guide that reveals some of Indiana's finest treasures. From parks to museums and other gems from all over the state, let *Short Indiana Road Trips* be your guide.

Short Indiana Road Trips

Table of Contents

Howard Steamboat Museum - Jeffersonville, IN – Page 1

Life on the Ohio River Historical Museum - Vevay – Page 4

Calli Nature Preserve – Page 7

Muscatatuck National Wildlife Refuge – Page 8

Big Oaks National Wildlife Refuge – Page 10

Muscatatuck Park – Page 14

Yellowwood State Forest – Page 17

A Visit to Pokagon State Park, Indiana – Page 19

Jackson-Washington State Forest – Page 23

Monroe Lake – Page 26

Garfield Park Conservatory and Botanical Garden -Page 36

Spring Mill State Park - Indiana History Comes Alive – Page 40

Falls of the Ohio State Park – Page 43

A Visit to Turkey Run State Park – Page 46

Visiting the Wilbur Wright Birthplace & Museum – Page 48

Bridgeton Mill, Bridgeton, Indiana – Page 50

Johnny Appleseed Park – Page 53

Wayne County Historical Museum – Page 57

Hillforest Historic Mansion – Page 59

Working Men's Institute – Page 61

Brown County State Park - Indiana's "Little Smokies" – Page 63

The Atterbury-Bakalar Air Museum – Page 70

Schimpff's Confectionery – Page 73

Indiana's Lost River – Page 76

Red Skelton Museum of American Comedy – Page 79

Hayes Arboretum, Richmond, Indiana – Page 83

Indy Canal Walk – Page 86

Foellinger-Freimann Botanical Conservatory Page - 89

Versailles State Park Page - 91

Visiting Nashville, Indiana Page - 95

Anderson Falls Page - 98

Indiana Military Museum Page - 101

Model T Ford Museum Page - 103

Indianapolis Artsgarden/Visitor Center Page - 104

George Rogers Clark Home Site Page - 106

Lanier Mansion Page - 110

Whitewater Canal State Historic Site Page - 114

About the Author – Page 120

Mossy Feet Books Catalogue – Page 121

Sample Chapter – Page 122

Sample –

Driving the Canals and Rivers Auto Trail

Franklin County Historical Marker - Metamora Grist Mill

Also in This Series

Fun Indiana Road Trips

Driving the Canals and Rivers Auto Trail

Parke County Covered Bridge Auto Trails

Batesville - Oldenburg Auto Tour

Short Indiana Road Trips

Howard Steamboat Museum - Jeffersonville, IN

Jeffersonville, Indiana lies along the banks of the Ohio River in southern Indiana. The spot, first occupied by white settlers who constructed Fort Finney near the current location of the Kennedy Bridge in 1786, quickly grew into a settlement. Fort Finney protected the area from American Indian attacks. They renamed the fort in 1791 to Fort Steuben in honor of Baron von Steuben, a Prussian general who served at Inspector General during the Revolutionary War, whom most military historians consider one of the fathers of the Continental Army. By 1793, there was no further need for the fort and the military abandoned it, but the city grew on.

Short Indiana Road Trips

22 Room Romanesque Revival Mansion

The old Howard family residence, a 22-room Romanesque Revival mansion, serves as the home of the Howard Steam Boat Museum. James Howard began his career of building boats in 1834 in Jeffersonville, Indiana on the Ohio River by establishing a boatyard and constructed his first boat, the Hyperion. His company would occupy three generations of his family and last 107 years. He had his home constructed next to the shipyard and used the craftsmen that worked on his boats to build his home in 1894. The work of these master craftsmen is evident throughout the home.

Examples of Master Woodworking Craftsmanship

There are several examples of these exquisitely crafted wooden fireplaces, as well as other finely built wooden features throughout the home as it exhibits grand staircases, carved window moldings and period furniture.

Delta Queen Paddlewheel

The museum includes many old steamboat artifacts, including items from Robert E. Lee, the Natchez, the Howard-built J. M. White and the pictured original paddlewheel from the Delta Queen.

Thousands of photographs, shipbuilding tools and implements and many paintings compliment the collection, affording the visitor a sense of the scale and importance of these successful enterprises.

Extensive Model Boat Collection

The model boat collection comprises dozens of steamboats, but includes many other types of historic watercraft that plied the waters of the Ohio, Mississippi and other of the rivers of the American interior. Water transportation was essential in the early years of the country and the Ohio was one of the major arteries, carrying passengers and freight along its course. Many of our immigrant ancestors rode boats like these to their new homes.

End of an Era

U.S. Navy Purchase for LST Construction

The Howard Steamboat Museum represents an important cog in our nation's history. The Howard family's control of the shipyard ended in 1941 when the U.S. Navy purchased the yard in 1941 to construct LST's for use during World War II. The Howard legacy and their contributions to Indiana's rich history continues today.

Howard Steamboat Museum

1101 East Market Street

Jeffersonville, IN 47130

(812) 283-3728

http://www.howardsteamboatmuseum.org/

Short Indiana Road Trips

Life on the Ohio River Historical Museum - Vevay, Indiana

Located in the quaint river town of Vevay, Indiana, the Life on the Ohio River, Life on the Ohio River Historical Museum will provide visitors with an insightful glimpse into the river life of the steamboat era, and before, of the folks that lived along this vital river. This small museum is packed with memorabilia from that bygone era. Visitors will find riverboat models, clothing, weapons and many other artifacts that depict life along the river.

Life on the Ohio River Historical Museum

208 E. Market St.

Vevay IN 47043

812-427-3560

http://www.switzcomuseums.org/files/River-History.html

swcomuseums@embarqmail.com

Switzerland County Historical Museum

The Switzerland County Historical Museum is located in southeastern Indiana near the Ohio River. The Switzerland County Historical Museum operates the Life on the Ohio River Historical Museum next door. The Switzerland County Historical Museum is located in a converted Presbyterian Church; the Ohio River Historical Museum is in the parsonage of the church.

Switzerland County Historical Museum

210 E Market St

Vevay IN 47043

Vevay

http://www.switzcomuseums.org

Swiss immigrants founded the town of Vevay in 1802, naming it after the Swiss city of Vevay from which they were native. Switzerland County was established in 1814 and Vevay was designated the county seat.

Early Settlement

The first settlers consisted of a man named John James Dufour who migrated to the United States in 1796. He settled in Kentucky and tried his hand at making wine. The venture failed and he searched for a better spot. He found one in the then Indiana Territory on the north side of the Ohio River. He obtained a tract of land from Congress and planted grapes near the current site of Vevay. The first wine was produced in 1806 or 1807. It was served to President Jefferson in the White House. Mr. Dufour's was the first successful commercial winery in the United States.

Swiss Wine Festival

The town celebrates this heritage each year during the last weekend in August with the Swiss Wine Festival.

http://www.swisswinefestival.org/

Transportation

Vevay Indiana is located on the banks of the Ohio River. Indiana State Road 56 crosses the city on a north/south axis, connecting Vevay with Rising Sun to the northeast and Madison to the west. Indiana State Road 129 creates a link with Versailles to the north and Indiana State Road 156 hugs the Ohio River from Patriot to Rising Sun. Vevay is located on the Ohio River Scenic Byway Auto Tour.

Scenic Byway – Southern Indiana Drive

http://ohioriverbyway.com/

Drive the 302 miles of scenic beauty along the Ohio River in Southern Indiana. The Ohio River Scenic Byway goes through historic communities, national forests and quaint villages. This wonderful drive through southern Indiana is a

Short Indiana Road Trips

wonderful experience and allows you to visit all the wonderful places in southern Indiana.

On its way across the state, it crosses Clark County, Dearborn County, Floyd County, Harrison County, Jefferson County, Ohio County, Perry County, Posey County, South Central Indiana, Spencer County, Switzerland County, Vanderburgh County, and Warrick County.

Food, Lodging and Shopping

Vevay is loaded with small town charm. Visitors will find several dining spots ranging from ice cream parlors, pizza spots, homey bars and restaurants. Those wishing to try their luck at the casino can visit nearby Belterra Resort. Stay at one of Vevay's bed and breakfasts or hotels. Visitors can also browse in any of the fine shops and art galleries located in the downtown area. For more information about Vevay, contact:

Switzerland County Tourism

128 W Main St

Vevay, IN 47043

812-427-3237

visitsc@switzcotourism.com

http://www.switzcotourism.com/

Calli Nature Preserve

Visiting Calli

To visit the Violet and Louis Calli Nature Preserve you will need to find County Road 40E. This road is about a mile east of downtown North Vernon, Indiana on US 50. The gravel road begins just east of the bridge across the Vernon Fork of the Muscatatuck River. After turning south on the gravel road, you will travel about a quarter mile to the parking lot, which is on the left. The road comes to a dead end at this point.

Dr. Louis and Violet Calli

Dr. Louis Calli and his wife Violet owned the land for the Violet and Louis Calli Nature Preserve. Dr. Calli was a physician who practiced for over fifty years in North Vernon. His wife Violet established the first Youth Center in North Vernon. She was awarded the Governor's Award for Community Service. The Jennings County Community Foundation owns the Nature Preserve. The Foundation manages the place in cooperation with the Indiana Department of Natural Resources.

The Nature Trailhead

The Violet and Louis Calli Nature Preserve consists of 180 acres. The trailhead for the self-guiding trail is adjacent to the parking lot on the same side of the road. The trail is just a bit over two miles long. There is a brochure available in a box at the trailhead that describes 18 stations along the course of the trail. There is also a notepad for you to register, just for fun.

The Trail

The trail begins with a pleasant stroll in the forest. It then follows the course of a spring fed stream. The best part of this hike is the extensive section that follows the course of the Vernon Fork of the Muscatatuck River. Some of the hike is along high bluffs overlooking the river. However, there are spots that allow access to sand bars extending out into the river. In early to mid April this portion of the trail is emblazoned with thousands of Virginia bluebells in full bloom. These flowers line the riverbank, the trail sometimes passing through vast beds of them. There are also some old hemlock stands along the river on these limestone bluffs.

Great Hike

The trail finishes up by passing through some open fields before finally exiting at the parking lot on the opposite side of the road. The Violet and Louis Calli Nature Preserve Nature Trail is a fun and pretty place to visit for a hike.

For more information, contact:

Jennings County Visitors & Recreation Commission

Box 215

Vernon, IN 47282

812-592-8087

http://www.jenningscounty.net/#!

Muscatatuck National Wildlife Refuge

Wildlife lovers should think about making a trip to Muscatatuck National Wildlife Area. The Refuge is on US 50 just east of Seymour, Indiana. The diversity of wildlife visible to even casual visitors to the Refuge is a delightful thing to see. The Refuge consists of 7,724 acres of which forestland covers about seventy percent. The remainder is wetlands managed by National Park Service personnel.

Muscatatuck River

The refuge takes its name from the Muscatatuck River that flows through the Refuge. The low, swampy area adjacent to the river forms the wetlands that make up the Refuge. The name Muscatatuck derives from an Amerindian word meaning "the land of the winding waters," an apt name for this rambling river. The river winds and rambles through the southern Indian countryside on its way to its mouth in the East Fork of the White River.

Wildlife at Muscatatuck National Wildlife Refuge

The best time to visit is in spring or fall because that is when the wildlife is most active. This is true especially of the waterfowl. These include a stunning variety of ducks, geese, grebes, great heron and other birds. Visitors can also, if lucky, watch the otters frolic in the waters and white tailed deer graze on the forest's edge. The Refuge manages a wide variety of habitat in Muscatatuck National Wildlife Refuge. There are grasslands, wetland and hardwood forests. Refuge personnel adjust the wetland waters seasonally to manage the plant species. They plant grain crops like corn to provide food for the animals and conduct periodic burns to control trees in the grasslands. Over 280 species of birds live or pass through in the Refuge, including a nesting pair of eagles that with luck a visitor might see.

Hiking

Hikers will enjoy hiking the eight trails, most of which are less than a mile in length. The two trails on the south end of the Refuge, the East and West River Trails are longer but close from time to time due to flooding. These two trails are not maintained as well as the others and hikers may find snakes along the marsh on the West River Trail. These trails travel along the Muscatatuck River for a portion of their lengths and will afford sightings of a nice variety of wildflowers. Visitors may also hike the maintenance roads that traverse between the marshes. Indeed, the hiker will find the greatest numbers of waterfowl and otters along these roads, as well as river otters cavorting in the placid waters. Morning and evening are the best times to visit, as during those times the birds and animals are most active.

Short Indiana Road Trips

Roads and Auto Tour

An auto tour along the marshy areas can yield a surprising number of heron, hawks and waterfowl, as well as white tailed deer. There are several pull off points for travelers to stop and view or photograph the wildlife.

Activities

Hiking, hunting, photography and fishing are the most popular activities at Muscatatuck National Wildlife Area. Small boats are permitted on some of the lakes; an Indiana State Fishing License is required for fishing. Hunters will need an Indiana State Hunting License and the appropriate stamps and tags. Boats can be either rowed or powered by an electric trolling motor.

Visitor Center

Before entering the Refuge, it is best to visit the Visitor Center. The center features a fabulous bookstore and a bird viewing area at the rear. There is also a new auditorium in which naturalists conduct wildlife programs. There are also clean restrooms at the Visitor Center. National Park personnel also hold special events and field trips throughout the year. For more information, calls the phone number listed below or visit the web site. This is an excellent place to visit to purchase books or pick up the self-guided auto tour and hiking trail map. Make sure you bring a picnic lunch, as there are many places suitable for a picnic. Nearby Seymour has a large variety of restaurants and grocery stores for supplies, as well.

Muscatatuck National Wildlife Refuge

12985 E. U.S. Hwyl 50

Seymour, IN 47274

812-522-4352

muscatatuck@fws.gov.

http://www.fws.gov/refuge/muscatatuck/

Big Oaks National Wildlife Refuge

Big Oaks National Wildlife Refuge began life as a test site for weapons during the opening days of World War 2. It has evolved into a unique wildlife haven in Southeastern Indiana. The Refuge, located near Madison, Indiana on US 421 is one of four National Wildlife Refuges found in Indiana. It served as a weapons testing site until the end of the Cold War in the 1980's. Only a very small portion of Big Oaks National Wildlife Refuge is currently open to the public. This is because large tracts of land contain unexploded ordinance. This ordinance is, of course, quite hazardous.

Military Weapons Testing

The 50,000-acre Nature Preserve occupies corners of three Indiana counties, Ripley, Jefferson and Jennings. Big Oaks is the largest of Indiana's three National Wildlife Preserves. The United States military opened the facility in 1940 for use as a weapons testing area. It saw extensive use during World War II, the Korean War and the Vietnam War. After the 1980's the facility's use began to wan and the military closed it in 1995. The Indiana Air National Guard still uses a 1000-acre parcel as a training range near the center of the property. Large areas of the preserve are off limits to the public due to the presence of unexploded ordinance. The cost to remove this ordinance is prohibitive, so it will remain. It is important when visiting Big Oaks to stay in public approved areas.

History of Big Oaks

After Indiana became a state in 1816, the Amerindian tribes that had occupied the land for hundreds of years had left. Small towns and farmsteads grew up in the rolling ground. It was a peaceful, rural area with no large cities close. During the middle years of the Civil War General John Hunt Morgan invaded the state. He crossed the Ohio River near

Short Indiana Road Trips

Corydon, Indiana. He crossed the southern Indiana landscape with his 2000 troops. Part of his route lay across the northern portion of Big Oaks. Two Union officers home on leave managed to capture two of his men within the confines of the Refuge. A monument marks the spot where they performed this deed. Hostilities in Europe and Asia in the late 1930's alerted the Army to the need to test more of its munitions. On December 6, 1940, the military announced its intentions to acquire land in southeastern Indiana. They chose this area because it was lightly populated and had nearby roads and rail lines. The military relocated over 400 families and began using it, now known as Jefferson Proving Ground, by the end of the year.

Wildlife Returns

Over the course of the military's use of the area, they surrounded it with a tall chain link fence topped by razor wire. Several military personnel and officers served at the base, which also employed many civilians in the area. Thus cut off, the land slowly reverted to forest and grassland and wildlife thrived. By the time the facility closed in 1995 huge tracts had reverted to the forest it had originally been. Deer, wild turkey and other wildlife thrived. After closing, debate over what to do with it occurred over the next few years. At length the government decided to turn it into a National Wildlife Refuge. Though the military still owns the land, the National Park Service manages the parcels within the Refuge. 200 species of birds, 46 species of mammals, 24 species of amphibians, and 17 species of reptiles are found on the refuge.

Visiting Big Oaks National Wildlife Refuge

The area around Old Timbers Lake in the northwest portion of the Refuge is the only area currently open to the public. It is a seventeen-mile drive from the Visitor Center. The Center is about seven miles from Madison, Indiana on US 421.

There are several miles of roadway around the lake, great for an afternoon drive or a day hike. Picnic areas are scattered around through Big Oaks National Wildlife Refuge. Hours are Monday and Friday 7:00 AM to 4:30 PM and the second and fourth Saturdays of each month. An admission charge is paid to enter the par. All visitors must view a safety video and sign an acknowledgement of danger form prior to entering the refuge.

Things to Do

Visitors may participate in several activities in the Refuge. Deer hunting and turkey hunting is permitted in designated areas during designated times. Anglers may fish in the 165-acre Old Timbers Lake. Bank fishing, only as boats are not permitted on the lake. Hikers can hike on the designated trails or on the many roads in the public area. Photographers will find many subjects for their camera, as the wild scenery in the Refuge is beautiful. Waterfowl and other wildlife will provide willing subjects. Refuge staff provides guided tours with advance reservation. There are several popular events scheduled throughout the year. See the website for informational brochures, event schedules and current hours of operation.

Big Oaks National Wildlife Refuge

1661 W. JPG Niblo Rd

Madison, IN 47250

https://www.fws.gov/refuge/Big_Oaks/about.html

Short Indiana Road Trips

Muscatatuck Park

Visitors will find Muscatatuck Park south of North Vernon on Indiana State Road 7 a wonderful place to visit. The picnic area at the Vinegar Mill Shelter offers a superb view of the Muscatatuck River below. In mid April to late May Trail 1 is a great place to find wild flowers along the river. It is also a superb hike during the cooler fall temperatures when the fall foliage in on the bluffs above the river is stunning.

The park offers seven miles of hiking trails on four trails. Many of the trails double as biking trails.

During warm days, many people enjoy frolicking and swimming in the Muscatatuck River. The park also has some shelters available for rent or on a first come, first serve basis. There are also playgrounds and basketball courts in the park. The public pool is only two miles away.

Muscatatuck Park History

Muscatatuck Park has an interesting history. Indiana purchased the property and established the fourth State Park there in 1921 as Vinegar Mills State Park. They named it for the stone cutting mill that existed there during pioneer times on the banks of the Muscatatuck River. The State changed the name in 1922 to Muscatatuck State Park. They drew the name from the winding river that wends its way through the Indiana countryside. During the 1930's, the Civilian Conservation Corps built many of the structures in the park. These include the road leading into the park, bridges, fire tower and the stone steps at the river overlook area at the Vinegar Mill.

Too small to serve as a State Park, the State decommissioned it and used the grounds to use it for quail and pheasant raising operations. This continued for a number of years until 1962. The State then used it for its new Youth Camp program. In 1967, the State offered to give the property to Jennings County to use as a park. After much discussion, the County took it. After the park deteriorated for several years, they began upgrades in the 1990's. The County moved the Walnut Grove One-room School there in 1991. They moved the Jennings County Visitors Center to the William Read Home in 1998.

William Read Home

William Read, the owner of the Vinegar Mill, built this home in 1850. Locally cut timbers make up the wooden frame. The stone foundation comes from stone cut from his stone cutting mill along the river. The brick were also made and kiln dried on the property. The State of Indiana used this home as a bed and breakfast inn during the time the park operated as a state Park. The Jennings County Visitors Center used the home for several years. The Jennings County Parks and Recreation Department uses it for offices now. The Visitors Bureau still keeps maps and other information there.

The Walnut Grove School

This school served students as a one-room schoolhouse in Sand Creek Township from the time of its construction in 1912. The Jennings County Preservation Association took up the monumental task of moving and renovating the school in 1990. They cut it into three pieces and moved it to the site it now occupies in Muscatatuck Park. It reopened in 1995 as a children's educational facility. They use it for an annual outing in which they dress in period clothing. They also get a lesson in pioneer life as it was in Indiana during its early days. The Preservation Association will open it for group or individual tours. The school has a library with old books, and other school items from its time as a schoolhouse.

Camping

The Campground has eight pull through sewer sites and twenty-six sites with water and electric. All sites have a fire ring and picnic table. There is a campground shower facility and there is a dumpsite at the campground entrance. Most of the campground is shaded.

Muscatatuck Park

325 North State Highway 3

North Vernon, IN 47265

812-346-2953

http://www.muscatatuckpark.com/

Yellowwood State Forest

Yellowwood State Forest has a lot to offer the outdoor enthusiast. A visit to Yellowwood will reveal trails to hike for the hiker, lakes to fish for the angler and forests to hunt for the hunter. Indiana State Forests are known as multi use properties. A number of activities take place there and they are a great place to visit during your vacation or weekend visit. With a gold panning, permit available at the Forest Office.

Picnicking

The picnic area at Yellowwood State Forest overlooks Yellowwood Lake. The pavilion is available to rent for family reunions, weddings or other events. Call the park office for rental information. There is a shelter with two fireplaces for cooking. Visitors will also find numerous picnic tables and fire rings for charcoal grilling. The grounds are well mowed and maintained. The surrounding Indiana forestland is a wonderful backdrop.

Hiking

Yellowwood Lake Trail surrounds Yellowwood Lake. It is about five miles long and goes through various habitats. Two sections pass through a fragrant pine forest. Yellowwood Lake Trail also passes through some magnificent forestland. It is about a two to three hour hike. Other trails include the four-mile Scarce O' Fat Trail and the one and one half mile Jackson Creek Trail. The Resource Management Trail is a one and one-half mile self-guiding educational trail. Pick up a brochure at the Park Office, just across the road. The forty-two mile Tecumseh Trail (http://www.hoosierhikerscouncil.org/tecumseh-trail/) also passes through Yellowwood.

This trail begins in Morgan-Monroe State Forest and traverses the Indiana countryside on its way to its trailhead in the Hoosier State Forest. Find more information about this trail at the link.

Fishing and Boating

Yellowwood Lake is open for fishing and boating. The DNR limits boat motors to electric trolling motors and anglers will need an Indiana State Fishing License. Since this is a mixed-use facility, hunters are allowed to hunt for deer, turkey, rabbits and squirrels.

Short Indiana Road Trips

Hikers should wear hunter orange during hunting season. Hunters will need a current Indiana Hunting license.

Horseback Riding

Equestrians will find a ten site primitive horseman's campground at Yellowwood. They will find around twenty miles of horse trails. "W" Horse Trail connects with the Brown County State Park trail system.

Camping

The Primitive Class C campground has about eighty sites. There are no shower facilities but there are vault toilets and running water nearby. There is also a carry in tent campground north of the Park Office. The Campground has a playground nearby.

Gold Panning

Budding prospectors can obtain a free gold panning permit to use at Yellowwood or at Morgan Monroe State Forests. The use of a pick, shovel or any other tool to displace soil is forbidden, but panning for gold is permissible, with the permit. Any archaeological like arrowheads, bones and pottery should be turned in to the office. For a permit, call if you cannot visit during opens hours. (812) 988-7945

Location

Yellowwood State Forest is about two miles off Indiana State Road 46, between Bloomington Indiana and Brown County State Park. It has several lakes and ponds as well as several hiking trails.

Yellowwood State Forest

772 South Yellowwood Road

Nashville, IN 47448

(812) 988-7945

http://www.in.gov/dnr/forestry/4817.htm

A Visit to Pokagon State Park, Indiana

Nestled in northern Indiana's lake country, Pokagon State Park has everything you would expect from an Indiana State Park. It also boasts some extras you might not expect. This Indiana State Park travel guide describes all the amenities of this popular state park. It also includes many of the wonderful attractions of Angola and Steuben County, Indiana. It also provides information about nearby Trine State Recreation Area. Pokagon State Park is also just a short distance from Nappanee, Indiana. Nappanee is the heart of the northern Indiana Amish country.

Potawatamie Inn

Potawatamie Inn is a large complex. It has many small nooks tucked away in odd places to relax with a book or a jigsaw puzzle, which all the inns have in abundance. Potawatomi is a one level facility. It has a swimming pool, dining room, great room with fireplace, gift shop and many other amenities. There is free wireless internet access in all the rooms and public areas.

Pokagon State Park Meeting and Conference Facilities

The resort at Pokagon State Park consists of 11,000 square feet spread out in nine meeting room. This conference center is the most popular resort in the Indiana State Park system. The Indiana State Park resort system is among the busiest state park system in the United States. Nine suites join the 137 guest rooms in the inn. The Inn's restaurant provides in house catering for banquets, conferences and other events.

Potawatomi Inn

6 Lane 100A Lake James

Angola, IN 46703

260-833-1077

http://www.in.gov/dnr/parklake/inns/potawatomi/

Short Indiana Road Trips

Lake James

This natural lake of 1,200 acres is Indiana's fourth largest natural glacial lake. James Watson Riley surveyed the area in 1831 a year after the native Potawotomi Indians left the area. Many think he named it after the males in his family named James, of which there were three. His father, he and a son all bore the first name, James. The lake includes three sections, the First, Second and Third Basins. Pokagon State Park borders all three sections, plus Snow Lake to the north, which connects to Lake James.

Camping - Cabins

Pokagon State Park has the full range of camping facilities available at Indiana State Parks. The facilities include:

Full Service Campground

Youth Campground

Group Campground

Full Service Campground

The campground is on the north side of the park just east of the Upper Basin of Lake James. There are 200 electric sites and 73 non-electric sites. The campground facilities include a picnic and fire ring at each site. Flush toilets, hot water and shower facilities located at convenient spots around the campground. There is also a dumping station. Reservations are available through the Central Reservation System.

Historic Cabins

Pokagon State Park offers seven historic cabins, each with a pair of double beds. Each rustic historic cabin at the park includes air conditioning, heat and a television. Maid service is also available daily.

Cabin Suites

Cabins suites at Pokagon State Park can sleep up to five people. The park offers four Cabin suites for overnight stays. Each cabin includes two queen beds and a single bed, plus a separate living room and dining room. Also, a cabin suite includes a coffee maker, microwave, compact refrigerator, two televisions, a table and chairs, and a writing desk

Hiking Trails at Pokagon State Park

Pokagon State Park has nine marked hiking trails that total eleven miles. The trails range from easy to moderate with most accessible from the Inn and campground.

Toboggan Run

The Toboggan Run allows riders to race down the hill for over 1700 feet on the refrigerated tracks. There are twin tracks, so two toboggans can run at a time. the toboggan Run has about 90,000 riders during the season. It features a ninety-foot drop and takes about forty seconds to complete. The highest recorded speed is forty-two miles per hour. The run is close to the inn. There is a heated refreshment building with hot drinks, sandwiches and snacks. Observers can sit inside watching the toboggans race downhill through the windows.

Skiing and Winter Sports

In addition to the toboggan run, other winter activities at Pokagon include sledding; ice skating, cross-country skiing (rental), camping and ice fishing.

Saddle Horses

Pokagon's saddle barn is open seasonally and offers rental horses and guided horse trail rides. There are hayrides on designated evenings. The bridle trail is two miles long and there is a shorter pony trail. There is no day use area for horses at this park.

Fishing

Lake James provides a wonderful place to fish, either from the bank or a boat. There is no public boat access at the park. However, visitors may fish from the fishing dock, from the bank or a rented boat availale at the boat rental station.

Pokagon State Park Swimming

Beach access at Pokagon State Park is free, but visitors do need to pay a gate fee to get in the park. There is a bathhouse with showers. The beach may close late in the season. It may also close when there is no lifeguard available to staff it. The beach opens the Saturday before Memorial Day and closed after Labor Day.

Picnicking

Picnic Shelters And Recreation Buildings

Pokagon State Park has picnic areas and shelters scattered around the park. Visitors may rent some of these shelters for family reunions, company functions, etc. To rent, visit this link.

Pokagon State Park offers a stunning variety of family freindly activites that range far beyond the scope of this article. For more information about the park and nearby Trine State Recreation Area, see the author's book, listed below. The book also includes several nearby attractions like Beechwood Nature Preserve and Marsh Lake Wildlife Refuge.

Jackson-Washington State Forest

Jackson-Washington State Forest comprises 18,000 acres in the beautiful "knobs" area of central-southern Indiana. The knobs, or as geologists call it, the Knobstone Escarpment, includes some of Indiana's most rugged terrain. It stretches from Brown County State Park in the north to the Ohio River in the south. Elevations range from 360 feet near the mouth of the Wabash River to Weed Patch Hill, which has an elevation of 1,056 feet above sea level. This hill is in Brown County State Park and is the third highest area in Indiana.

Multi-Use Facility

Jackson is a multi-use property. Hunting, fishing and trapping is permitted. The State of Indiana conducts periodic timber sales in the State Forests. The monies obtained by the sale of licenses, fees and timber go into the Heritage Trust fund that the State uses to procure more property. The State began acquiring the land that now encompasses Jackson-Washington in the 1930's. The other activities offered at

Jackson-Washington are camping, hiking, boating, fishing and horse trails.

Skyline Drive

Skyline Drive in Jackson-Washington State Forest is about two miles south of Brownstown, Indiana on Indiana State Road 250. Turn right off the State Road on Skyline Drive. At the top of a steep grade, visitors will find the first of five overlooks. The drive is about three miles long before Stare Holler Road branches off to the left on its way to another Department of Natural Resources facility called Starve Hollow Lake. The knobs tower over the surrounding area providing some spectacular vistas. Skyline Drive and the area around it boast some fabulous vistas that afford some magnificent fodder for an autumn foliage drive.

Camping

The campground at Jackson-Washington is on the east side of Indiana State Road 250. It is a few miles south of Brownstown, Indiana. It is a (Class C) campground, meaning it is primitive. There are pit toilets, no electricity, hot water or showers. The campground charges a nominal fee, paid at the park office. There are some waterfront sites on Knob Lake, but most are located in the bordering fragrant pine forest. Campers may purchase firewood at the park office during normal business hours. There is also a youth campground for youth groups to use.

Fishing

There are five lakes at Jackson-Washington for anglers to try their luck. The facility allows boats with electric trolling motors only on Spurgeon Hollow Lake and Knob Lake. Anglers will need an Indiana State Fishing License. Spurgeon Hollow Lake has wheelchair accessible fishing docks.

Hiking

Many of the trails at Jackson Washington State Forest are challenging trails, as the knobs terrain has steep hills. The eleven trails range from one mile to eight miles. The Backcountry Trail is the longest at eight miles and is located near Starve Hollow Lake in the Forest. Hikers will find the other trails in the main area south of Brownstown on Indiana State Road 250 on the left side of the highway just past the turnoff for Skyline Drive. This area is where the camping, hiking, picnicking, fishing take place.

Hunting

Jackson-Washington provides hunting for white-tailed deer, ruffed grouse, eastern wild turkey, rabbit, quail, dove, squirrel, fox, coyote, and raccoon in designated areas. An Indiana State Hunting license is required.

Horse Trails

Jackson-Washington State Forest has about fourteen miles of trails. The parking area for the horse trails is a few miles further south on SR 250, past its intersection with Indiana State Road 39.

Picnicking

There are also several great places to picnic in the Forest. The Forest has five total shelters available for rental (Skyline Drive, White Oak, and Pinnacle). There are two oven shelters (Skyline and CCC playground). Picnickers will find ten total picnic areas scattered around the Forest.

Jackson-Washington State Forest

1278 East State Road 250

Brownstown, IN 47220

(812) 358-2160

http://www.in.gov/dnr/forestry/4820.htm

Short Indiana Road Trips

Monroe Lake

Monroe Lake, at 10,750 acres, is the largest lake in Indiana. The lake is southwest of Brown County State Park, southeast from Bloomington and accessible from Interstate 69 on Indiana State Road 37. Boaters can enjoy fishing, waterskiing or just relaxing on the lake. Campers can stay at any of the Paynetown State Recreational Area. Visitors will also find beaches, hiking, hunting and picnicking opportunities at Lake Monroe.

Beaches

Beach swimming is available during open hours from Memorial Day through Labor Day. Beach bums will find two beaches. They are in the Paynetown and Fairfax recreation areas. The bathhouses at both locations provide showers, dressing rooms, restrooms, and food concessions for visitors to the lake.

Hunting

All hunters are required to register at check-in stations daily. Hunting in Waterfowl Resting Areas is by special permit only. Deer, grouse, turkey, squirrels, doves and rabbits are the primary game species. Excellent waterfowl hunting is available during the season. Waterfowl hunting information is available at Paynetown Visitor's Center.

Interpretive Naturalist Services (Seasonal)

Explore the world of natural resources while enjoying interpretive and recreational programs. Program schedules are available at Interpretive Services.

Boating / nine Launch Ramps

Boaters will find ramps at nine locations around the lake. The boat launch ramps are not marked on the map but are listed under the facilities.

Fishing / Ice Fishing

The lake has bass, bluegill, catfish, crappie, walleye and hybrid stripers. Anglers need an Indiana State Fishing License. Visitors may purchase these at the Park Office. There are fishing piers located at various places on the lake.

Hiking

Hikers will find easy to moderate marked trails open for hiking all year. Off-road uses of vehicles, bicycles and horses are not permitted.

Description of Hiking Trails

Bluebird Trail (1.25 miles) Moderate—this is a forest and field trail in Paynetown State Recreation Area.

Tree Trek Trail (0.5 mile) Easy—this is a forest Ecosystem interpretive trail in Paynetown State Recreation Area.

Turkey Trot Trail (1.75 miles) Moderate

Short Indiana Road Trips

There is a Hike-In/Boat-In Camping Area in Allen's Creek State Recreation Area.

Whitetail Trail (1 mile) Moderate—this trail provides access trail for walk-in visitors at Paynetown State Recreation Area.

Picnicking / Shelter house

Picnickers can find lakeside picnic areas and shelters in several areas. Most of these areas have tables, grills, toilet facilities, a playfield and shelter. Reservations for shelters are available through the Central Reservation System. http://indianastateparks.reserveamerica.com/

Boat Rental - Fishing Boats, Pontoons

Lake Monroe Boat Rental

Pleasure Craft Marina

Boat owners will find seasonal mooring on docks or buoys. These mooring docks are at Paynetown, Moore's Creek, Cutright and the Fairfax Recreation areas. Other services provided at Fairfax, Cutright and Paynetown include fuel, food and rental boats. Paynetown and Fairfax provide pump-out stations.

Camping

The campground is located at the Paynetown State Recreational Area. Campers will find 312 campsites consisting of 222 AAA sites. They have electricity, modern restrooms showers, picnic table and grills. There are also ninety non-electric sites.

Electric / 226 sites

Non-electric / 94 sites

Camp Store (Seasonal)

Dumping Station

Fourwinds Resort and Marina

Fourwinds Resort and Marina is located on the shores of picturesque Lake Monroe. It is just west of Fairfax State Recreation Area. The Fourwinds Resort & Marina has tennis courts, miniature golf, boat ramps, indoor/outdoor pool and a marina. There is no hiking at Fairfax but you may fish and walk the grounds. The resort offers a variety of amenities, including:

Indoor/Outdoor Heated Pool

Boat Rentals

Private Beach

Fitness Center

Tennis Courts

Mini-Golf

Basketball

Volleyball

Board Games

Marina

Fishing

Hiking & Walking trails

Hunting

Nearby 6,700 yard, par 71-championship golf

Weekend entertainment during summer months

A complete fleet of watercraft rentals from jet skis to party boats,

The Windjammer Grill

Tradewinds Restaurant

Lakeside beach

Mini-golf

Short Indiana Road Trips

Regularly scheduled live entertainment

Scenic brick paths bordering the lake

Fourwinds Resort and Marina

9301 Fairfax Road

Bloomington IN 47401

812-824-2628

http://www.fourwindsresort.com/

Fairfax State Recreational Area

Fairfax includes the following features:

Beach and Bathhouse

Boat Launch

Boat Rental

Lodging

Marina and Fuel

Picnicking

Playground

Restrooms

Showers

Store

Drinking Water

Fairfax State Recreational Area

9301 South Fairfax Road

Bloomington, IN 47401

Phone: (812) 837-9546

Salt Creek SRA

Boat Launch

Restrooms

Pine Grove State Recreation Area

Pine Grove Road

Bloomington IN

Pine Grove State Recreation Area is a great place for birding. Warblers, shore birds, vireos, waterfowl and even eagles may be spotted here.

Crooked Creek State Recreational Area

Crooked Creek Road/Dewar Ridge Road

Boat Launch

Restrooms

Paynetown State Recreational Area

Paynetown is located off Highway 446. This state operated area on the northeast side of Lake Monroe has electric and non-electric camping. Visitors will also find a boat rental service, a marina with gas sales and a camp store. The DNR-staffed Interpretive Center is located near the park entrance. Entrance fee or state park pass required.

Bloomington IN 47401

(812) 837-9546 (812) 837-9967

(Accessible)

Beach w/Bathhouse

Boat Launch

Boat Rental

Camping

Hiking Trails

Interpretive Naturalist

Marina -• Fuel

Short Indiana Road Trips

Picnicking

Playground

Restrooms

Showers

Store

Visitors - Nature Center

Drinking Water

Hiking

Three short trails

Nature Trail

Whitetail Trail (1 mile) Moderate — this is an access trail for walk-in visitors at Paynetown State Recreation Area.

Blue Bird Trail

Forest and Field Trail

1.25 miles - Moderate

Tree Trek Trail

Forest Ecosystem Interpretive Trail

0.5 mile-Easy

Waterfork Waterfowl Nesting Area

South Axsom Branch Road

From Indiana State Road 46 turn south on Steele Road, pass the TC Steele home. Turn right on Gilmore Ridge Road. Turn left on Deckard Ridge Road. Left turn on South Axsom Branch Road. The area is closed from October 1 to April 1.

Northfork Waterfowl Resting Area

McGowan Road

The area is closed from October 1 to April 1.

From Bloomington, go east on State Road 46 to Kent Road. Go west from Brown County State Park, through Nashville. This is a gravel road just before the bridge over Salt Creek. Turn right onto Kent Road and follow it across a bridge to McGowan Road. Turn right onto McGowan Road and follow to the Stillwater marsh overlook and the North Fork area.

Open October 15 through April 15; the rest of the year there are viewing stations to watch waterfowl. Bald eagles have been sighted.

Parts of the NorthFork complex are closed from October 15 through April 15. Hunting is permitted in the Stillwater/North Fork area. This area is excellent for waterfowl, raptors, shorebirds, and wading birds.

Stillwater Marsh

McGowan Road

To get to Stillwater Marsh from Bloomington, go east from Bloomington on State Road 46 to Kent Road. Go west from Brown County State Park through Nashville. This is a gravel road just before the bridge over Salt Creek. Turn right onto Kent Road and follow it across a bridge to McGowan Road. Turn right onto McGowan Road and follow to the Stillwater marsh overlook and the North Fork area.

Stillwater Marsh is open October 15 through April 15; the rest of the year, there are viewing stations to watch waterfowl. There have been bald eagles sightings here, also.

During the winter and early spring, DNR staff pumps water into Stillwater from the north fork of Salt Creek. This creates an important resting area for waterfowl. In mid-April, they drain the marsh and sow wildlife food crops. The result is a rich habitat area for animals of all types.

Parts of the NorthFork complex are closed from October 15 through April 15. Hunting is permitted in the Stillwater/North Fork area. This area is excellent for waterfowl, raptors, shorebirds, and wading birds. Birding enthusiasts can expect to find the following birds at Stillwater Marsh:

Swans

Geese

Grebes

Ducks

Flycatchers

Olive-sided

Yellow-bellied Flycatchers

Acadian Flycatchers

Vireos

Veery Thrush

Gray-cheeked Thrush

Wood Thrush

Cerulean Warbler

Yellow-throated Warbler

Worm-eating Warbler

Prothonotary Warbler

Kentucky Warbler

Hooded Warbler

Louisiana Waterthrush

Bald Eagles

Northern Harriers

Southfork Marshes

Blue Creek Road

The Southfork Marshes are on the eastern end of Lake Monroe. The waters of Lake Monroe overflowing the banks of Sand Creek due to the dam form them.

Monroe Lake

4850 South State Road 446

Bloomington, IN 47401

(812) 837-9546

http://www.in.gov/dnr/parklake/2954.htm

Short Indiana Road Trips

Garfield Park Conservatory and Botanical Garden - Indianapolis Indiana

The 136-acre Garfield Park Conservatory and Botanical Garden is the oldest of the Indianapolis city parks. Designed by German landscape architect George Edward Kessler, the sunken garden opened on October 29, 1916.

History of Garfield Park Conservatory and Botanical Garden

Garfield Park sprang from two unsuccessful attempts to operate a racetrack and fairgrounds from an area known as Bradley Woods. The Jeffersonville Railroad owned the area and sold it to a group in 1888 that opened the Southern Riding Park. This venture failed, and Marion County Sheriff N. R. Rucker. He later sold the property to the City of Indianapolis. The city leased to a group called the Indiana Trotting Association. Their venture failed also, due to the area's remoteness from the city. The city transformed the land into a park, calling it Southern Park in 1876. The city renamed the park Garfield Park in 1881, in honor of the recently assassinated President James A. Garfield. The city extended the streetcar line to the park in 1895. Numerous improvements took place at the park until Indianapolis hired German landscape architect George Edward Kessler to design a new park.

Southern Riding Park

George Edward Kessler (July 16, 1862 – March 20, 1923)

The son of Edward Carl Kessler and Adolphe Clotilde Zeitsche Kessler, George was a native of Frankenhausen, Germany. The family immigrated to the United States in 1865. The family lived in several states before settling in Dallas, Texas. Edward died when George was sixteen. His mother, in consultation with relatives, decided that George would work in landscape architecture. She took him back to Germany to study at the Grand Ducal Gardens in Weimar, Germany. Kessler studied there and at various other places in Europe before returning to the United States in 1881. He obtained his first design job in Johnson County, Kansas designing Merriam Park. During his lifetime, he completed over 200 projects and prepared plans for 26 communities. He designed twenty-six park and boulevard systems, 49 parks, 46 estates and residences, and 26 schools. Kessler did several projects for Indianapolis including a park and boulevard system in 1909. Indianapolis has named Kessler Boulevard in his honor.

This article excerpted from the author's book:

Exploring Indiana's Historic Sites, Markers & Museums - Central Edition

http://mossyfeetbooks.blogspot.com/2016/05/exploring-indianas-historic-sites.html

Conservatory

Kessler spent the next several years designing and building the park. Construction of the first conservatory completed in 1915. This conservatory lasted until 1954. The Park constructed the current structure to replace it. This 10,000 square foot conservator was the first to use welded aluminum and glass construction in the United States. It houses a luxuriant tropical habitat featuring tree frogs, koi, free flying birds and a fifteen-foot waterfall. Visitors will also find cacao plants, banana trees, fig trees, and an extensive orchid collection. Plant lovers will find a host of other plantings that can turn a cold winter day into a tropical vacation. The conservatory staff hosts changing educational displays as well as three floral displays each year.

Sunken Gardens

The Sunken Gardens include a three-acre formal classical European garden. The brick walkways, fountains, and extensive plantings provide a restful place to walk in a serene setting. Visitors may enjoy three main floral displays in the Garfield Park botanical garden. The spring tulip display peaks about mid-April. The summer annual flower display is usually best from June through August. September and October is when the fall mum display takes place.

Picnic Areas - Pagoda

Garfield Park has ample places to picnic with tables and shelters scattered throughout the park. Visitors will also find playgrounds for children to play and plenty of walking paths.

Garfield Park Arts Center

The Arts Center utilizes arts spaces, visual arts galleries, classrooms and a literary arts library to provide city residents with a diverse artistic and cultural experience. The galleries are open to the public and are free to view.

Garfield Park Arts Center

2432 Conservatory Drive

(317) 327-7135

Memorials, Events, Field Trips and Tours

In addition to the numerous memorials, trails and sports facilities, visitors will find numerous events, field trips and tours hosted by park staff. For more information, contact:

Garfield Park Conservatory

2505 Conservatory Dr.

Indianapolis, IN 46203

(317) 327-7183

http://garfieldgardensconservatory.org/

MacAllister Center for the Performing Arts

Visitors will find numerous events and concerts hosted at the MacAllister Center for the Performing Arts. For information, contact:

http://www.indy.gov/eGov/City/DPR/Programs/Arts/Pages/GarfieldParkArtsCenter.aspx

MacAllister Center for the Performing Arts

2432 Conservatory Drive

Indianapolis, IN 46203

http://garfieldparkindy.org/index.php?id=88

Short Indiana Road Trips

Spring Mill State Park - Indiana History Comes Alive

Space age and pioneer history collide at Spring Mill State Park. The park's pioneer village depicts frontier life in the nineteenth century. The Gus Grissom Memorial celebrates the life of a local space age hero, Gus Grissom, an astronaut who participated in the Mercury and Apollo Space Programs. These two facilities combine to relate the history of this interesting area. The many attractions at the park include:

Spring Mill Pioneer Village

Hiking and Mountain Bike Trails

The Spring Mill Inn

Gus Grissom Memorial

Modern and Primitive Camping

Twin Cave Boat Tour

Spring Mill Pioneer Village

The park's main feature is the restored pioneer village. The village includes over twenty log structures and an operating water wheel that powers a gristmill and sawmill. During the summer months, park staff dressed in nineteenth-century garb, run a loom, a blacksmith shop and a potter's shop. Artisans also create leather and wooden items using period tools. Visitors may watch the gristmill grind corn and see the sawmill cut boards from logs, all with waterpower from the robust stream that passes through the park. A garden demonstrates plants that the pioneers grew for food and medicine. Visitors may ask the gardener about the various crops that the villagers grew.

The Spring Mill Inn

The Spring Mill Inn provides comfortable rooms and a great room with a fireplace for people to read, play games or just relax. The inn's dining room serves breakfast, lunch and dinner to residents of the hotel and the public. Guests will also find an indoor/outdoor pool and banquet facilities for events.

Modern and Primitive Camping

The campground includes both modern and primitive camping facilities. There are almost 200 modern sites with electricity and fire rings. The campground also has showers and restrooms. Primitive campsites do not have showers, modern bathrooms or electricity but do have fire rings.

Gus Grissom Memorial

The space program defined America in the 1960s and the drive to be the first nation to put a man on the moon gave pride to the entire country. This program produced its own set of heroes. One local hero, Gus Grissom, gave his life for this effort. Hailing from nearby Mitchell, Indiana, he flew in the second Mercury mission on July 21, 1961. His death occurred during a pre-launch practice for Apollo 1 on

January 27, 1967. The Memorial contains Grissom's Gemini III capsule, helmet, spacesuit and other NASA artifacts. Visitors do not need to pay a state park entrance fee to visit the Memorial as it is just outside the main gate. Trail 6 begins and ends near the Memorial. This handicap accessible paved trail goes through a portion of the Donaldson Nature Preserve.

Twin Cave Boat Tour

Available from Memorial Day through Labor Day, the boat tour travels five hundred feet into Twin Cave. This memorable tour allows visitors to see cave creatures.

Hiking and Mountain Bike Trails

There are almost 10 miles of hiking trails at Spring Mill State Park ranging from rugged to easy. Most of these trails traverse through forested areas. There is a two-mile mountain bike trail near the Camp Store where visitors may rent mountain bikes.

Wonderful Vacation

If you are looking for a memorable vacation spot, Spring Mill State Park could fit the bill. With nature, history, comfortable lodging and dining facilities the park is a wonderful place to spend a week or a weekend. For park information, call (812) 849-4129.

A *Visit to Spring Mill State* Park provides the potential visitor to the area with all the information needed to assure a fun, memorable vacation.

http://mossyfeetbooks.blogspot.com/2015/08/a-visit-to-spring-mill-state-park.html

Falls of the Ohio State Park

This, the smallest Indiana State Park, is part of the Ohio National Wildlife Conservation Area. The park resides in the town of Clarksville, Indiana just across the river from Louisville, Kentucky. The State of Indiana established the Falls of the Ohio State Park to preserve the fossil beds that lay exposed on the exposed riverbed.

Falls of the Ohio Visitor Center

The visitor center is the best place to begin a visit to Falls of the Ohio State Park. The Visitor Center occupies the site of the former Camp Joe Holt, a Union Camp during the American Civil War. The camp served as a major troop staging area for Union troops invading the Confederate States of America. Unlike other State Parks, Falls of the Ohio is not accessible using the State Park Pass. The fees serve to reimburse the City of Clarksville for building the Visitor Center.

Falls of the Ohio State Park Visitor Center

The Visitor Center at Falls of the Ohio State Park contains scores of fossils, highlighted by the massive mammoth skeleton mounted in the main entrance. The fossils include examples of fossils found in the fossil beds on the grounds and in southern Indiana. The Interpretive Center at Falls of the Ohio is a family friendly facility. It displays a plethora of information about the history of the river area. The Falls area includes the Indiana towns of Clarksville, New Albany, Jeffersonville, and Louisville, Kentucky across the river. This area is rich in history. Before the installation of the locks, riverboats had to stop at the Falls. The passengers and cargo had to be portaged around them. The cities played an important role in this process. Jeffersonville blossomed into an important riverboat-building center and rail hub. The area served an important role during the Civil War. Terry Chase, a well-established exhibit developer designed the

Visitor Center with its many easy to understand exhibits in 1990.

Riverbed Exposed - Fossil Beds

The 390-million-year-old fossil beds at Falls of the Ohio State Park are among the largest, naturally exposed, Devonian fossil beds in the world. There is a trail here, The Woodland Loop Trail, which has ten new stainless steel markers denoting the plant life of the trails completed by area Eagle Scouts. The visitor may tour at will or take a guided tour. Careful examination of the riverbed will reward the visitor with many unusual fossils. State Law forbids collecting the fossils. Take only pictures. The best time to visit is from August to early November when the river levels are traditionally low. The Falls of the Ohio no longer exist, hidden under the McAlpine dam, but the exposed fossil beds provide a fascinating window into the past.

A Visit to Falls of the Ohio State Park

A Visit to Falls of the Ohio State Park will guide the visitor to Falls of the Ohio State Park on their visit to this wonderful area. In addition to the Park, visitors will find many other attractions in one of Indiana's earliest settled areas. Lewis and Clark set out on their renowned journey to the northwest coast from the Falls of the Ohio area. Visitors can visit George Rogers Clark's home site, where the trek started, as well as other fun places to visit in Clark and Floyd counties.

The book Falls of the Ohio State Park is part of the Indiana State Park Travel Guide Series. This series will encompass all the family friendly Indiana State Parks. Indiana's State Park system is one of the finest in the United States. With great hiking trails, history, and nature, there is something for everyone at an Indiana State Park.

A Visit to Falls of the Ohio State Park

http://mossyfeetbooks.blogspot.com/2015/09/falls-of-ohio-indiana-state-park.html

Falls of the Ohio State Park

201 W Riverside Dr.

Clarksville, IN 47129

Area: 165 acres (67 acres)

Phone: (812) 280-9970

http://www.in.gov/dnr/parklake/2984.htm

Turkey Run State Park

Turkey Run State Park is the second state park established in Indiana in 1916. Two covered bridges, the Cox and the Narrows Covered Bridge on either end of the park provide a scenic backdrop to many wonderful photo opportunities in the park. Visitors may stay either in the large campground or in Turkey Run Inn with its accompanying restaurant. Park visitors may fish, with an Indiana license, in Sugar Creek and hikers can enjoy the many miles of great hiking.

History

Established in 1916 as Indiana's second state park, Turkey Run is on Indiana State Road 47 about two miles ast of its intersection with US 47. The state acquired the property from the Hoosier Veneer company for $40,000 after receiving a $20,000 grant from the Indianapolis Motor Speedway.

Sugar Creek Canoeing

Sugar Creek bisects the 2382 acres of rugged woodland terrain, providing some wonderful off site canoeing opportunities which span two state parks. A suspension bridge connects the developed south section with the wild north section. Canoeists will find Sugar Creek an excellent place to canoe. Turkey Run State Park does not have a canoe or boat rental; however, visitors will find a number of private canoe rental companies that run Sugar Creek. Canoeists will find a public access site on the south end of the park at the Cox Ford Bridge.

Turkey Run Inn

The Turkey Run Inn has seventy-nine rooms, a heated pool, and a large, cozy sitting room with a fireplace. The rooms range from cabins to suites that include a Jacuzzi tub.

Camping

The 213-site campground is equipped with flush toilets, hot water and showers. Most sites will accommodate trailers. No individual water or sewer hookups, but electricity is available.

Hiking

Turkey Run has eleven hiking trails that total fourteen miles. Most of the hiking is quite rugged with the trails passing through some wild, heavily forested canyons and hills. Some hug the banks of Sugar Creek, affording some spectacular views of the creek and the Narrows Bridge. Others wind precariously up damp, beautiful valleys, and then climb through forestland.

Horseback Riding

Many State Park Saddle Barns offer riding lessons, scout badges, gift certificates, birthday parties, corporate outings, campfire programs and other services. The Turkey Run Saddle Barn offers hayrides and guided horseback rides. The Barn is open from April through October, weather permitting. Riders cannot bring their own horses. The park has many miles of horse trails and the facility offers differing riding packages of various lengths. Currently the escorted ride packages are for a one-mile and a four-mile ride. Reservations are suggested for hayrides.

Other Activities at the Park

Visitors will find a host of other activities at the park like picnicking, swimming, tennis and other outdoor sports. Turkey Run State Park is located in beautiful Parke County, which offers the largest concentration of covered

Turkey Run State Park

8121 E. Park Road

Marshall, IN 47859

(765) 597-2635

http://www.in.gov/dnr/parklake/2964.htm

http://www.coveredbridges.com/

Short Indiana Road Trips

Visiting the Wilbur Wright Birthplace & Museum

The Wilbur Wright Birthplace and Museum affords visitors an excellent place to learn about one of Indiana's most famous native sons, Wilbur Wright. The Wright family had extensive ties to the Hoosier state, having resided at various places in Indiana during Orville and Wilbur's formative years. The home is the site of Wilbur Wright's birth. It is where he spent his early childhood.

Wilbur Wright (April 16, 1867 – May 30, 1912)

His father Milton and mother Susan moved a lot while Wilbur was a child due to Milton's job. When Wilbur was two, the family moved from Indiana to Dayton, Ohio. Here, in 1871, Orville Wright was born. It was during their stay at Dayton that Milton brought home a toy helicopter in 1878 that enthralled the two boys. This toy helicopter spurred the boy's interest in their quest to fly. In 1881, the family moved to Richmond, Indiana where Wilbur attended high school. During this time, the boys had tried to build flying helicopters from the model their father had given them. These did not fly well, so the brothers began building kites. Wilbur had accrued enough credits to graduate, but their sudden move back to Dayton prevented him receiving his diploma. He planned on going to college at Yale, but his mother became sick with tuberculosis and he stayed home to care for her.

Flight Experiments

After stints in the printing and bicycle repair and manufacturing businesses, the brothers return to studying flight from after learning of Octave Chanute's glider experiments on the shore of Lake Michigan near Miller Beach, Indiana. The Wrights based their design on Chanute's biplane glider he tested there.

The Wilbur Wright Home

The house on the site is not the original home in which Wilbur Wright was born. The house was constructed in 1845 and purchased by Milton in 1865. The home went through several owners and renters by the time the State of Indiana purchased the home on April 21, 1929 it was in a state of disrepair. The state razed the house in 1955, replacing it with a monument. Efforts at reconstruction began in 1971 when archeologists located the original foundation. Workers constructed the present house in 1973 using materials and design elements of the original house as much as possible. On November 3, 1995, the State of Indiana deeded the property to the Wilbur Wright Birthplace Preservation Society. The home is furnished with period furniture, many original to the Wright family.

The Museum

Adjacent to the home visitors will find a fabulous museum that includes photos, memorabilia and artifacts from the Wright brother's quest for flight. The museum has a reproduction of the Wright brothers bicycle shop in Dayton and the shops nearby. Visitors can also visit a reproduction of the camp the brothers set up at Kitty Hawk to conduct their experiments. The only full size reproduction of the Wright Flyer built to fly is also on display in the museum. The museum is self-guided; however, the visitor will find numerous signs, charts and other informational material to afford an educational and enjoyable tour. The staff does offer guided tours for school groups, buses and other groups.

Wilbur Wright Birthplace & Museum

1525 N. 750 E.

Hagerstown, IN 47346

(765) 332-2495

wilbur@nltc.net

http://www.wwbirthplace.com/

Bridgeton Mill, Bridgeton, Indiana

Bridgeton is on Bridgeton Road about nine miles south of its intersection with High Street in Rockville, Indiana.

Joseph Lockwood and Isaac J. Sillman built a sawmill just south of the 10:00 Line in 1823 on Raccoon Creek. They would later add a burrstone to grind grain. Daniel Kalley and a James Searing purchased the mill in 1837 and added a distillery. The mill and distillery burned down in 1845. By 1868 another mill, the current one, was built.

Bridgeton 1878 House

Originally the home of the miller, the structure now serves as the location of gift shop that offers unique gifts, antiques and handcrafted merchandise.

1822 Case Log Cabin

One of the oldest cabins in Parke County, the cabin was the home of the Seba Case family. The adjacent 1878 Barn is available to rent for weddings and other events.

Conley Ford 1907 Covered Bridge

Built by bridge builder J. Lawrence Van Fossen in 1907, many believe the 192-foot long bridge is the fourth longest single span covered bridge in the world. Located east of Bridgeton spanning Raccoon Creek, the bridge is still open to automobile traffic.

Bridgeton Covered Bridge

J.J. Daniels built the original 267 foot long bridge in 1868 for $10,200. The bridge was a 2-span covered Burr arch-truss design that spanned Little Raccoon Creek. The bridge closed to traffic in 1967. An arsonist destroyed the bridge in 2005. Local residents reconstructed the bridge the following year.

1892 Iron Bridge

Constructed by the Wrought Iron Bridge Company in 1892 across Big Raccoon Creek, this historic iron 175 foot long bridge, now bypassed, is northeast of Bridgeton on Mansfield Road.

For more information on the history, shops and dining in Bridgton, contact:

Historic Attractions

Bridgeton Covered Bridge Association

http://www.bridgetonindiana.com/

8227 S. Bridgeton Road

P.O. Box 77

Bridgeton, IN 47836

Phone: (765) 548-4095

Short Indiana Road Trips

Bridgeton Grist Mill

http://bridgetonmill.com/

Perched on the banks of Raccoon Creek, Bridgeton Grist Mill is the oldest continually operating gristmill in Indiana. The mill has been open at some point in every year for over 180 years. It is not the oldest gristmill in Indiana, but no other mill has been in continuous operation for that long. The mill began as a log sawmill that eventually included a gristmill as well. That mill burned down in 1869. The mill reopened in a new building, after conversions to a roller mill in the 1880's and to an electric mill in 1951. In 1969 new owners converted it back to a gristmill with the installation of 200-year-old, forty-eight inch French Buhr Stones. This family owned mill is continually being updated and improved. The picturesque mill stands beside the pretty Bridgton Covered Bridge which spans Raccoon Creek over the dam that provides the gristmills power.

The Bridgton Covered Bridge Festival occurs annually in mid-October and runs for ten days. There are other festivals throughout the summer.

For more information, contact:

Bridgeton Grist Mill

8104 Bridgeton Rd

Bridgeton, IN 47836

(812) 877-9550

bridgetonmill@gmail.com

http://bridgetonmill.com/

Johnny Appleseed Park

This thirty-one acre park on the northeast side of Fort Wayne serves as the final resting place for Johnny Appleseed. The park is home to the annual Johnny Appleseed Festival in September. Visitors will find many other recreational activities in the park as well. These include St. Joseph River access, camping, a dog park and picnicking.

John Chapman (Johnny Appleseed) (September 26, 1774 – March 18, 1845)

The son of Nathaniel Chapman and Elizabeth Simonds Chapman, John was a native of Leominster, Massachusetts. His mother died giving birth to a son, who died about two weeks after his mother. Nathaniel had enlisted in the Continental Army. He was away at war when his wife died. Historians know little of Chapman's early life. He and his eleven-year-old brother migrated west into the Northwest Territory in 1792. The two boys lived a life in the wilderness until their father migrated into the new state of Ohio in 1805. Apparently, at that time, John apprenticed to a nurseryman who tended apple trees. Thus began Chapman's lifelong career.

Johnny Appleseed Businessman

Most of the legends that surround Johnny Appleseed, the nickname that people gave him, involve him randomly planting apple seeds in the frontier. The truth is far different. Chapman foresaw that the frontier would expand west. By planting the apples, he established a claim on the land on which they were planted. He moved ahead of the wave of settlement, planting apple tree seeds, a valuable commodity on the frontier. Thus, by the time he died in 1845 he had accumulated over 1200 acres land. By the time the apple trees were ready to sell to incoming pioneers, the pioneers had arrived to buy them.

Short Indiana Road Trips

Johnny Appleseed Nurseryman

Chapman moved through the wilderness, choosing his land carefully. Once he found choice spots, he would clear a section, fence it and plant his seeds. Every couple of years he would return to the site to tend the seedlings. He worked mostly in the states of Ohio, Pennsylvania and Indiana. When the pioneers arrived near his nursery, he would sell off the trees, then much of the land. He sold his seedlings for three cents each, seven cents if he wanted the buyers to allow him to plant them. The apples he planted were not the familiar types found in grocery stores and orchards today. These apples were hard, tart and nutritious. Pioneers used them to make cider, applejack, apple butter and other frontier staples.

Missionary

Chapman was a devout Christian and a member of the Church of Swedenborg, known as the New Church. During his travels, he served his church as a missionary, spreading his message to isolated pioneer homesteads, where he frequently boarded, and to the natives he encountered as he traveled. He would spend his evenings at a homestead spinning stories and telling about his faith. His beliefs spurred his celibacy. Chapman never married, believing that God would reward his abstinence in heaven.

Death at Fort Wayne

Chapman lived in the Fort Wayne area from the mid-1830's until his death in 1845. His orchard about twelve miles south of Fort Wayne, on the banks of the Maumee River, held around 12,000 trees. He died in Fort Wayne in 1845 and is interred in Johnny Appleseed Park at Fort Wayne.

St. Joseph River Access

Located on the banks of the St. Joseph River anglers and pleasure boaters can enjoy access via the Indiana Department of Natural Resources approved boat ramp.

Camping

Located along the banks of the St. Joseph River, the campground offers close access to Fort Wayne's downtown attractions as well as to the river. The campground normally opens in mid April and remains open until October 31, closing only during the Johnny Appleseed festival.

Park Campground

1500 E Coliseum Boulevard

Fort Wayne, IN 46805

Camp Canine

Opened in 2000, the dog park expanded in 2010 to include a Dog Agility course to aid dog owners in training their dogs as well as provide an exercise facility for them. All dogs need to have a Pooch Pass to enter the park. For more information about the dog park, contact:

Fort Wayne Parks & Recreation Department

Administrative Office

705 East State Street

Fort Wayne, Indiana 46805

(260) 427-6000

Camp Canine

Picnic Area and Playgrounds

http://www.fortwayneparks.org/index.php?option=com_content&view=article&id=104&Itemid=169

Short Indiana Road Trips

Park visitors will find ample picnic tables along the river and a large playground for the kids.

Johnny Appleseed Park

1500 E Coliseum Blvd

Fort Wayne, IN 46805

(260) 427-6720

(260) 427-6000 - Off Season

http://www.fortwayneparks.org/index.php?option=com_content&id=173:johnny-appleseed-park&Itemid=33

Johnny Appleseed Festival

http://www.johnnyappleseedfest.com/

Wayne County Historical Museum

The compact site includes eight historical buildings with a wealth of historical photos and artifacts from Wayne County's history. The Museum hosts several special events throughout the year. This museum represents itself as a miniature Smithsonian Museum. The description is far from deceptive. The visitor can expect to spend a minimum of three hours in this delightful museum.

Miniature Smithsonian

The museum covers a wide spectrum of subjects, using a vast array of models, artifacts, photographs and documents. History, geology, archeology, aviation, transportation and agriculture are just a few of the topics the visitor can expect to find in the museum.

Early Life in Indiana

Wayne County Historical Museum includes a magnificent array of exhibits that interpret the early history of Richmond and Indiana in general. The exhibits include maps, documents, models and artifacts that display many of the items and methods the pioneers and early residents used to complete their daily tasks. Visitors can learn and enjoy examining the rich array of artifacts and models in the museum.

Egyptian Mummy

The Sarcophagus Room has an Egyptian mummy complete with sarcophagus. Archeologists believe the man died around 900 BC. Read about him and the fascinating story of the woman that acquired him, Julia Meek Gaar.

Vintage Automobiles

Just when the visitor thinks they have completed their tour of the museum, they enter the vintage automobile section in the huge garage. The display includes many automobiles manufactured right in Richmond.

Wagons and Carriages

Upon exiting the rear of the museum, the visitor will next find an impressive assortment of wagons and carriages. The assortment includes a milk wagon, hearse, carriages and a school hack. A number of horse drawn agricultural equipment is found in this area.

Palladium Printing Office

Founded by Nelson Boone, the grandson of Squire Boone and great nephew of Daniel Boone, the Richmond Palladium began publishing in 1831 in Richmond. The Wayne County Historical Museum includes the complete print shop, including type cases and printing presses from this early newspaper.

A Multitude of More

Visitors will also find a log cabin, general store, vintage furniture and much more. For more information, contact:

Wayne County Historical Museum

1150 North A Street

Richmond, In, 47374

http://www.waynecountyhistoricalmuseum.org/

Hillforest Historic Mansion

Hillforest sits on a bluff overlooking the Ohio River. Designed by architect Isaiah Rogers and constructed by industrialist and financier Thomas Gaff in 1855, Hillforest Mansion sits astride a hill that affords a majestic view of the Ohio River.

Thomas Gaff (July 8, 1808 - April 25, 1884)

The son of James and Margaret Wilson Gaff, Thomas was native to Edinburgh, Scotland. His father, a paper maker, moved the family to Springfield, New Jersey. Gaff received his education in private schools and learned papermaking from his father. An uncle, Charles Wilson, taught him the distilling business. Thomas and his brother James founded a distillery in Philadelphia. In 1843, the brothers moved their operation to Aurora, Indiana. Their distillery, called the T & J.W. Gaff & Company Distillery, produced bourbon, rye, and Thistle Dew Scotch whiskey. The business thrived and their business empire expanded to include the Crescent Brewing

Company, a Nevada silver mine, farming operations and many others. The Gaffs also owned a fleet of steamboats that they used to transport their various products on the rivers.

Isaiah Rogers (August 17, 1800 – April 13, 1869)

The son of Isaac and Hannah Ford Rogers, Isaiah was native to Marshfield, Massachusetts. A student of famed Massachusetts architect Solomon Willard, Isaiah became a leading architect in the United States. He designed structures in Mobile, Alabama, Boston, New York City, Louisville, Kentucky, and Cincinnati, Ohio. His designs included Boston's Tremont House, New York's Astor House and the Burnett House in Cincinnati.

Hillforest Historic Mansion

Situated on ten acres of land overlooking the Ohio River, Gaff lived in the home until his death in 1884. The Gaff family retained ownership of the home until furniture manufacturer Will Stark purchased the home in 1924. The local chapter of the Veterans of Foreign Wars owned the home, using it as a meeting place, until a group of local citizens purchased the home in 1955. Organizing as the Hillforest Historical Foundation, the group restored the home and opened it for public tours in 1956. The National Historic Landmark Program listed it as a National Historic Landmark in 1992. The restored home is open for tours from April 1 until December 30. The home was designated a National Historic Landmark in 1992.

Hillforest Historic Mansion

213 Fifth St

Aurora, Indiana

812-926-0087

http://www.hillforest.org/

Working Men's Institute

Philanthropist William Maclure established the Institute in 1838. The Working Men's Institute inhabited a wing in the Harmonist Church until 1894. In that year, it moved to this impressive building three-story structure on Tavern Street. The Institute at one time comprised 144 Institutes in Indiana and additional sixteen in Illinois at its height. The Working Men's Institute has dwindled to this location. This is the oldest continuously operating library in Indiana. Their founding mission was the dissemination of useful knowledge to working men and their families. That remains their mission today.

William Maclure

William Maclure (October 27, 1763 – March 23, 1840)

A native of Ayr, Scotland, MaClure first came to the United States in 1778. He started as a businessman and traveled in Europe. He traveled to France in 1803 to try to collect debts incurred in the United States during the French Revolution. While in Europe, he began to study geology and became fascinated by it. Upon his return to the United States, he made a geological survey of the country. His work earned him the nickname, "Father of **American Geology.**"

The New Harmony Experiment

He became acquainted with Robert Owen when he visited Owens's cotton mill in New Lanark, Scotland. He met with Owen again in 1825 and decided to join him in his New Harmony experiment. MacClure joined the "Boatload of Knowledge" that traveled to New Harmony, arriving on the boat Philanthropist in January 1826. From New Harmony, he traveled to Mexico where he died in 1840. The terms of his will set up a trust that established 160 workingman's institutes.

Maclure served as the State of Indiana's first State Geologist. He purchased the Rapp-Owen Granary to use as a museum and laboratory. He was also instrumental in organizing the Working Man's Institute

The Museum

This building serves as a library and museum. The museum fills three rooms on the second floor. There is an elevator up to the museum from the entry room, which is quite impressive. The museum, small as it is, contains a wealth of local artifacts and information. Visitors should budget a couple of hours for the museum. The exhibits include both the skeleton and story of a horse called Old Fly that had an interesting history. Serving his rider in the Civil War, Old Fly died a ripe old age here in New Harmony.

The Library

The Library serves patrons in New Harmony, Harmonie Township and the members of Alexandrian Public Library in Mount Vernon, and the Poseyville Carnegie Public Library in Poseyville. Services include public computers, photocopies, fax machine. The library charges a fee for copy and fax services. Tax and voter registration forms are also available at the library. The library also includes the Branigin Archive and the Lilly Archive. The Branigin Archive includes documents and records from the two communal societies that operated in New Harmony, the Harmonists and the Owenites. The Lily Archive is an extensive collection of rare books. Books from William Maclure, David Dale Owen, Richard Owen, Robert Dale Owen, as well as other prominent figures are included in the Archive.

The Working Men's Institute hosts several events throughout the year. For more information, contact:

Working Men's Institute Museum & Library

407 Tavern Street

New Harmony, IN 47631

(812) 682-4806

http://workingmensinstitute.org/

Short Indiana Road Trips

Brown County State Park - Indiana's "Little Smokies"

Lovely vistas, great hiking and horseback riding are just three reasons to visit Brown County State Park. Near Nashville, Indiana this 15,000 state park has so much to offer it is impossible to take it all in on a one-day visit. That is okay, because if you wish to stay longer the park has an inn, a campground and housekeeping cabins.

Stay the Night at Abe Martin Inn

The eighty-four room Abe Martin Lodge is the centerpiece of the park. The inn has a dining room, indoor water park and swimming pool as well as a recreation room and conference facilities. There is wireless internet service throughout the inn. There are also twenty-four motel type cabins near the inn.

1405 State Road 46 West

Nashville, IN 47448

(812) 988-4418

http://www.in.gov/dnr/parklake/inns/abe/

Indiana State Park Housekeeping Cabins

The park maintains twenty housekeeping cabins. These cabins provide comfortable accommodations for visitors to the park. These two bedroom cabins sleep eight people. Each has a living room, kitchen, bathroom, linens, dishware and cooking utensils.

Camping at Brown County State Park

The variety of camping facilities at the park includes:

Electric - 401 Class A sites

Non-Electric - 28 sites

Rally - 60 sites

Horsemen's Campground

Electric - 118 sites

Non-Electric- 86 sites

Youth Tent Areas

Class A sites have electricity and water connections. The campground has a camp store, flush toilets and hot water showers. The campground is open year round. The Horseman camp has two sections, electric and non-electric. The 118 site electric section has extra large sites that accommodate horse trailers. There is a shower house and several pit toilets. The seventy-nine site primitive campground has pit toilets. There are no shower facilities or flush toilets in the primitive campground.

Horse Barn and Riding Trails

In addition to the horseman campground, Brown County State Park has a horse barn where park visitors may rent horses by the day or the hour. The park has over seventy miles of horse trails.

Short Indiana Road Trips

Hiking and Biking Trails

Hikers can enjoy ten trails totaling twelve miles of trails that rank from moderate to rugged. There are also two short, easy self-guided nature trails. Mountain bikers have twelve miles of trails weaving through the forested hills.

Drive Brown County State Park - Auto Tour

The park contains over twenty miles of paved road. Several overlooks provide stunning vistas of the park.

Picnic at the Park

The park has an abundance of picnicking possibilities. There are several shelters available for rent or casual use. There are picnic areas with restrooms and playgrounds throughout the park. Picnic tables occupy many of the secluded areas of the park, also.

Boating and Fishing

Anglers can fish in either of the parks two lakes and rowboats may use Ogle Lake.

Swimming at the Pool

Brown County State Park has an Olympic-size pool located near the north entrance, just off Indiana State Road 46.

Other Facilities at Brown County

Besides all this, the park has additional activities that include:

Tennis Courts

Open Fields

Playground Equipment

Brown County State Park Auto Tour

The six-mile self-guided auto tour at Brown County State Park provides an excellent way to spend a quiet summer afternoon. The park contains over twenty miles of paved road. In the southern portion of the park, visitors will find a self-guiding auto tour loop. During the summer months, Brown County State Park offers a self-guided auto tour of the park with cassette tape. Inquire at the Nature Center for the tape.

Ramp Creek Covered Bridge

Ramp Creek Bridge is not on the auto tour, but it is at the north entrance of Brown county State Park and is the first thing visitors see as they enter the park. Ramp Creek is Indiana's oldest covered bridge built in 1838 by Henry Wolf. It is the only Double Tunnel Bridge in Indiana and one of four in the United States. The DNR moved it from Putnam County in 1932 from its location on Ramp Creek. It now crosses Salt Creek at Brown County State Park. It is a single span burr arch truss design. The bridge is 110 feet long, including 7-foot overhangs. The portal width of both lanes is eleven feet wide and twelve feet high.

The bridge is listed on the National Register of Historic Places

The bridge is on the North Gate Entrance and all vehicles must go through it. Tall vehicles or cars with bikes on top may not make it through. If your vehicle will not clear, you will have to use the West Gate Entrance located west of Nashville on Highway 46.

Many consider Brown County State Park to be the premier state park in Indiana. With its varied activities, wonderful facilities and scenic vistas, who is to say that they are wrong? A visit to Indiana's "Little Smokies" is sure to delight everyone.

Short Indiana Road Trips

To contact the park for more information:

Mailing Address:

Brown County State Park

P.O. Box 608

Nashville, IN 47448

(812) 988-6406

http://www.in.gov/dnr/parklake/2988.htm

Nashville

Little Nashville Indiana is located in the scenic hills of south central Indiana at the intersection of Indiana State Roads 46 and 135. It is about a mile west of Brown County State Park. Nashville is the county seat of Brown County.

While not a large town, Little Nashville is chuck full of shops, restaurants and coffee houses making it a delightful place to visit. Most of the buildings are patterned after early American architecture. Some are original log cabin structures, others are reproductions. It resembles Gatlinburg, Tennessee, only smaller.

The shops offer merchandise not found in the big box stores. Some of the offerings are handcrafted, made locally. A local winery maintains a shop in the village, as well as numerous antique and art galleries, candle and gift stores. To find them all, you must peruse every little alleyway and street, as the stores are tucked in every conceivable corner.

For more information about Nashville and Brown County, contact:

Brown County Convention & Visitors Bureau

P.O. Box 840

10 North Van Buren St.

Nashville, IN 47448

800.753.3255

http://www.browncounty.com

Short Indiana Road Trips

The Atterbury-Bakalar Air Museum

The Atterbury-Bakalar Air Museum honors the memory of the service people that served at the base.

Atterbury Army Air Field

Captain Stratton O. Hammon had broad authority over the laborers, suppliers and railroads that transported materials to the new base when construction commenced in the summer of 1942. He had more than 1000 workers employed during the construction, which lasted until February 1943. The 2000-acre base cost over four million dollars to construct the over one hundred buildings. The primary use was to train B-25, B-26, and glider pilots. The Wakeman Hospital served as a medical care center for wounded World War II soldiers and later during the Korean War. The base was renamed in 1954 to honor Lieutenant John Bakalar. The base closed in 1970.

Brief History

The task of organizing the mammoth task of constructing the airfields needed to train 70,000 pilots annually fell to General of the Army and General of the Air Force Henry Harley "Hap" Arnold. He moved the responsibility of building air bases from the overburdened Quartermaster Corps to the U. S. Army Corps of Engineer. The Army had no plan for any of the bases, only a set of guidelines that followed General Arnold's concept of "Spartan" simplicity for the bases. There would be no frills or creature comforts at these bases. The buildings would be simple lumber and tar paper construction. These buildings were quite cold in winter and hot in summer. The hangers were of wood or concrete. The guidelines called for one secure hanger to hide the Norden bombsight, which was top-secret. Atterbury's construction followed these guidelines during its construction. The United States, in the face of major war, needed a multitude of air bases and it needed them fast. The site that Atterbury would occupy had been open cornfields. This land needed to be turned into a United States Army Air Field as quickly as possible.

Short Indiana Road Trips

Lieutenant John Bakalar (August 29, 1920 - September 1, 1944)

The son of John Bakalar, Jr. and Marie Wills, John was native to Hammond, Indiana. Bakalar enlisted in the United States Army Air Corps at Fort Harrison, Indiana on January 26, 1942. On May 3, 1944, Bakalar joined the 353rd Fighter Squadron, 354th Fighter Group in Europe. This group was known as the "Pioneer Mustang Group," as it was the first to receive the powerful North American P-51 Mustang fighter-bomber. Bakalar took part in various bombing and strafing missions in France, supporting Allied troops there. He completed forty-five combat missions, receiving the Air Medal with three oak-leaf clusters for his bravery. His squadron would receive the Presidential Unit Citation. During his first combat sortie on August 16, 1944, he won three aerial victories. Bakalar would die on September 1, 1944 when the engine on his plane failed shortly after takeoff, sending the airplane crashing into the forest. Visitors can view the stone and bronze plaque erected in his honor at the entrance to the museum.

The Atterbury-Bakalar Air Museum

The Atterbury-Bakalar Air Museum preserves the memory and history of this airfield. Located on site, the museum is a treasure trove of memorabilia, history and exhibits covering the Atterbury Army Air Field and Bakalar Air Base.

Atterbury-Bakalar Air Museum Military Memorabilia

The Atterbury-Bakalar Air Museum is located near the control tower across the street from the F4C Phantom Jet Fighter static display at the Columbus Indiana Municipal Airport. This is the former location of the Atterbury Army Air Field and Bakalar Air Force Base. The museum is just a few steps from the ramp and control tower.

This small, but intense museum contains a plethora of models, artifacts and photos relating to the history of Bakalar Air Base and the Atterbury army camp. It is well worth the few hours time that it takes you to browse the museum. For more information, contact:

Atterbury-Bakalar Air Museum

4742 Ray Boll Boulevard

Columbus, Indiana 47203

(812) 372-4356

http://www.atterburybakalarairmuseum.org/

Short Indiana Road Trips

Schimpff's Confectionery

History

Bavarian widow Magdalene Schimpff dispatched her twelve-year-old son, along with his uncle, to the United States to investigate possible places to settle. Louisville had a large German community, thus the family chose to settle there. The pregnant Magdalene, with her five children migrated to Louisville sometime before the Civil War. She and her daughters established an embroidery business, while the sons opened a confectionery store. One of Magdalena's sons, Charles, opened a confectionery store across the Ohio

River in Jeffersonville around 1871. The store was successful for almost twenty years until Charles decided to close it.

Gustav A. Schimpff Sr. (1843–1918)

Gustav had worked at a local confectionery business, the C.G. Block & Company during this period. This business evolved into the Wurach & Bergreen Company. Schimpff bought a share of this company in 1871. This company closed in 1889 and Schimpff started working for the Frank A. Menne Company, another leading confectioner. After Charles closed his store in Jeffersonville, he urged Gustav to open one in Jeffersonville, as his had been quite successful. Thus on April 11, 1891 Gustav, along with his son, Gustav Jr., opened a confectionery store at the current location at 347 Spring Street. It is the only candy store in Indiana that has operated continuously for over 125 years.

Museum

In addition to the wonderful variety of candies made right in the store, the owners have on display in the store thousands of artifacts of American candy memorabilia. The collection has taken decades of work to acquire and display. Visitors will delight at the vast array of old time store displays, candy tins, dispensing machines and signage.

Products

The signature candy is the Cinnamon Red Hots, first made by Gustav in 1891. Customers can watch as workers make Modjeskas, hard fish candy and other sweet treats behind the counter.

Tours

Interested visitors can arrange for a tour of the store conducted by Jill Schimpff. She can accommodate up to forty people on the free tour, which includes a candy making demonstration and tour of the store. Although the store, Candy Demonstration Area, Chocolate Dipping Room, and Candy Museum are always open during normal store hours, the only way to guarantee that the candy making process is in operation is to book a tour in advance.

Schimpff's Confectionery

347 Spring Street

Jeffersonville, IN 47130

(812) 283-8367

http://www.schimpffs.com/

Short Indiana Road Trips

Indiana's Lost River

The Lost River in Orange County constitutes one of Indiana's most unusual geologic features. The river dives underground, pursuing its course through a subterranean system of channels as it courses its way to its rendezvous with the East Fork of the White River south of Shoals, Indiana

The Lost River

Length - About 87 Miles

The Lost River is a large sinking and subterranean stream, and an intricate cave system. There are two forks of the Lost River. The North Fork begins southwest of the intersection of North Smedley Road and West Ben Walton Road. The South Fork of the Lost River begins about 1.5 miles south just west of North Smedley Road in Washington County. The North and South Forks of the Lost River meet about three miles west of their sources. The junction is somewhat less than a mile east of Claysville, IN, just south of Lost River Road in Washington County. On its way, west the Lost River crosses Washington, Orange and Martin Counties. For about 23 miles of this length, mostly in Orange County, the Lost River flows underground, hence its name. Many of the features are on county roads that are not hard to find. The uniqueness of the Lost River makes is worthwhile to find them. The main features include the Wesley Chapel Gulf and the Orangeville Rise.

Wesley Chapel Gulf

Wesley Chapel Gulf is a 187-acre tract of land located on the Hoosier National Forest in western Orange County, Indiana. It is named for the Wesley Chapel Church, located just to the north. Visitors will find Wesley Chapel Gulf about four miles southwest of Orleans and two miles east of Orangeville. To find, drive south from Orleans on Indiana

State Road 37 to County Road 490 N, about 2.4 miles. A sign pointing towards Orangeville marks the road. Drive west on CR 490 (CR 500 at some point) for about 3.6 miles, reaching County Road 350 W. The Wesley Chapel Church marks the intersection. The church was built in 1858, originally known as Bruner's Chapel, and has an associated cemetery. The Gulf derives its name from the church. Turn left (south). The parking lot for the Wesley Chapel Gulf is about one half mile south of the church. A Hoosier National Forest sign indicates the correct spot to park. A short hiking trail leads to the Wesley Chapel Rise.

Wesley Chapel Gulf received designation as a National Natural Landmark in 1972 due to its impressive geologic features. The gulf provides a rare glimpse of the Lost River on its subterranean path. Several other karst features are represented in the immediate area of the Gulf including swallow holes, sinkholes, and caves. The Forest Service recognized the uniqueness of Wesley Chapel Gulf and acquired the property in 1996 through a land exchange with U.S. Gypsum Co. The best time to visit Wesley Chapel Gulf is in the fall after the foliage has died down, or during the winter months.

Orangeville Rise

From Wesley Chapel Gulf, return to County Road 500 N and turn left (west). County Road 500 N becomes first CR 525 N, then CR 540 N before intersecting County Road 500W. Turn left (south) towards Orangeville. The parking area is on the south side of Orangeville. A short trail leads to the Rise.

At the Orangeville Rise Indiana's second largest spring comes to the surface, forming streams that intersect with the Lost River a short distance away. The Rise is a tributary of the Lost River that rises from a cave into a 220-foot diameter rock-walled pit. The stream formed flows southwest to merge with the Lost River. The 355 square mile watershed of the Lost River covers five counties. This area possesses a large number of underground caves, sinkholes and underground streams.

The Indiana Karst Conservancy owns the three-acre area.

Tours

Forest service personnel conduct tours from time to time. For information, contact:

Visit French Lick West Baden

8102 West State Road 56

West Baden IN 47469

866-309-9139

http://www.visitfrenchlickwestbaden.com/

Tour on your Own

Visitors may tour on their own at any time. For more information, contact:

Wesley Chapel Gulf

http://www.fs.usda.gov/detail/hoosier/about-forest/?cid=fsbdev3_017567

Hoosier National Forest

Indiana Karst Conservancy

PO Box 2401,

Indianapolis, IN 46206-2401.

http://www.caves.org/conservancy/ikc/

Division of Nature Preserves

402 W. Washington St., Rm. W267.

Indianapolis, IN 46204.

317-232-0209.

http://www.in.gov/dnr/naturepr

Red Skelton Museum of American Comedy

Red Skelton was an iconic performer in the middle of the Twentieth Century. His long running television show was required watching on millions of American television sets from 1954 until 1970. His comedy spanned every medium available at the time, radio, television and stage. He was not just one of the funniest men ever to perform; he was also a talented painter and writer.

Red Skelton (July 18, 1913 – September 17, 1997)

The son of Ida Mae Fields and Joseph Elmer Skelton, Richard Bernard Skelton was native to Vincennes, Indiana. His grocer father had been a clown in the Peru based Hagenbeck-Wallace Circus, the second largest circus in the United States during its heyday in the early Twentieth Century. Joseph died shortly before Red's birth. The family was poor, and Red began selling newspapers at an early age to make money for the family. Local legend suggests that Red's interest in show business stemmed from an incident involving Ed Wynn, a popular comedian at the time, who was performing in Vincennes. Wynn purchased every paper the boy had, and then took him on a tour of the show, even taking him backstage to introduce him to the performers. Red had to ability to make people laugh an extremely young age. He began performing skits at minstrel shows and a showboat, the Cotton Blossom.

Beginning of a Career

Skelton quit school at age thirteen and ran off to pursue a show business career. His mother let him go with her blessing. He started performing in burlesque shows and then graduated to vaudeville. He met Edna Stillwell at a dance marathon. The two would marry and have one child. Edna became his writer. Skelton gained fame and gained an invitation to perform at one of President Franklin D.

Roosevelt's luncheons. By 1938, he obtained his first movie contract. His movie career lasted until 1956.

Radio

His first radio appearance was on the Rudy Vallée's The Fleischmann's Yeast Hour in 1937. He appeared with fellow Hoosier Joe Cook. Their performance led to two repeat performances later that year. He would get his on radio show, The Raleigh Cigarette Program, in 1941. Red developed many of the characters he would continue to use during his later television career. Clem Kadiddlehopper, The Mean Widdle Kid and others came to life under the Red's talented craft.

Divorce and Drafting into the Army

His marriage to Edna ended his married man deferment. Now classified 1-A, the army drafted him, which forced the network to cancel his popular radio show. The army placed him in the entertainment corps. He would perform ten to twelve acts a day to entertain the troops. The strain caused his health to decline. He spent time at a military hospital recovering form exhaustion and mental breakdown. The strain left him with a stuttering problem. While recovering he befriended a soldier that was expected to die. Red started trying to make the man laugh. He succeeded. The man recovered, and in the process, Red's stuttering problem disappeared.

Return to Radio and then Television

The army discharged him in 1945 and he returned to radio. He added more characters to his repertoire, including Cauliflower McPugg, Deadeye and San Fernando Red. The new medium of television started becoming popular. Red landed a television contract in 1954. For a few years, Red worked in television, radio and movies simultaneously. The workload became too great and his last movie was a flop.

His Red Skelton Show on television would run until 1970. In spite of good ratings, CBS cancelled the show.

Later Career

Skelton returned to the stage in the latter years of his career. He performed live performances in theaters, nightclubs and at college campuses. He also appeared in numerous television specials.

Red Skelton Art and Short Stories

Red began painting clowns in 1943. He did not show his work, considering it a hobby. His second wife, Georgia, persuaded him to show his art during one of his performances in 1964. He sold several paintings as well as reproductions and prints. Some estimate that Skelton made more money from his paintings than he did with his television shows. He also wrote one short story a day for many years. In addition, he penned many songs and symphonies. An avid gardener, he designed his own Japanese and Italian gardens.

Red Skelton Museum of American Comedy

The Red Skelton Museum of American Comedy is a testament to the humor, art and music of Red Skelton. This fabulous museum includes five-minute video clips of Red Skelton's characters along with the props and costumes he wore while performing the skits. The museum spans Skelton's entire vaudeville, radio, movie and television career. Several pieces of Skelton's art are also on display as well as some of his books and music he composed.

Red Skelton Museum of American Comedy

20 W Red Skelton Blvd

Vincennes, IN 47591

(812) 888-4184

http://www.redskeltonmuseum.org/

Red Skelton Birthplace

The Red Skelton Birthplace is located directly across from the Red Skelton Performing Arts Center & Museum of American Comedy. His birthplace has been purchased by the Red Skelton Foundation to preserve an important part of his life but additional funds are needed to restore the home. Donors who would like to be a part of preserving and presenting the Red Skelton life story may contact:

Red Skelton Birthplace

111 W. Lyndale Avenue

Vincennes, IN 47591

http://www.redskelton.com/

Hayes Arboretum, Richmond, Indiana

Hayes Regional Arboretum is located on the northeast side of Richmond Indiana just a short distance from I-70 or US 40. The arboretum features a museum, arboretum, guest quarters, nature center, Adena and Hopewell Indian mounds, ponds, fields, and wetlands and trails for hiking. The 466-acre property contains a portion of virgin, old growth forest, one of the few such stands in Indiana. Visitors can hike, take an auto tour, watch birds or bike during a visit to the Arboretum.

Dairy Barn Nature Center

The Nature Center offers plenty to do for an afternoon's relaxation. A bird viewing room is equipped with comfortable chairs and a large window overlooking a bird feeding station. Birds of all kinds and squirrels can be seen actively feeding at the various types of bird feeders. The Nature Center is located in an old renovated dairy barn that was originally constructed in 1833.

History Tree

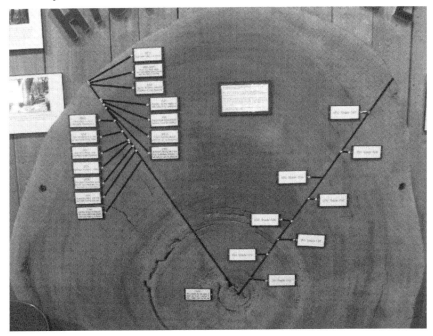

This huge sycamore tree stood in an area due to be flooded by the Brookville Reservoir. Removed before the waters covered it, scientists determined that the twenty-two foot diameter tree was well over 400 years old. Labels on the tree indicate events that occurred at different stages of the trees life.

Bird Watching Room

Visitors may watch an impressive variety of wildlife in climate controlled comfort of the bird watching room. Many species of birds, squirrels, chipmunks and other animals visit the feeders to feed.

Bee Hive

Upstairs in the Nature Center you will find an active beehive filled with honeybees. Watch them as they build wax cells and produce honey for their winter's food.

Herb Garden

Learn your herbs at the Arboretum's impressive herb garden. The plants have tags identifying them.

Nature Walks

Hikers will find five trails totaling three miles of hiking trails that wind through different forest habitats. There is also an auto tour, for which there is a nominal fee to use. The funds collected assist in the maintenance of the facility.

Old Growth Log

The 466-acre Hayes Arboretum contains 3% of Indiana's old growth forest. Hikers will find a huge preserved log that is a reminder of the vast forests that once covered the Hoosier State.

Museum

Visitors may also visit a small museum containing artifacts from the founder of Hayes Arboretum, Stanley Hayes.

Membership

If you purchase a membership in Hayes Regional Arboretum, you also have access to the Hayes House. This facility may be used as an overnight accommodation, site for weddings or meetings and other group functions.

Hayes Arboretum

801 Elks Country Club Rd

Richmond, IN 47374

(765) 962-3745

http://www.hayesarboretum.org/

Short Indiana Road Trips

Indy Canal Walk

The Indy Canal Walk begins near the Indiana State Museum and travels along the old Indianapolis Central Canal past three museums, White River State Park and past upscale apartment and condominium buildings that face the canal. Hikers and bikers can visit the Medal of Honor Memorial, ride a paddleboat or gondola or just enjoy the magnificent view of Downtown Indianapolis from the walkway. The loop, which travels along both sides of the canal, is about three miles long. Major attractions along the canal include:

Indiana State Museum

Eiteljorg Museum

Indiana History Center

White River State Park

Medal of Honor Memorial

The Central Canal

Authorized by the Mammoth Internal Improvements Act, the canal's purpose was to connect Indianapolis with the Wabash and Erie Canal, thus providing a water access point to the Ohio River at Evansville. Workers only completed about eight miles of the canal before financial difficulties forced construction to come to a halt.

Indiana State Museum

The Indiana State Museum complex includes 40,000 square feet and well over 450,000 artifacts. The Museum also houses the Indiana Store, the IMAX Theatre and numerous special exhibitions throughout the year.

Indiana State Museum and Historic Sites

650 W. Washington St.

Indianapolis, IN 46204

317-232.-1637

http://www.indianamuseum.org/

Eiteljorg Museum

This exciting museum displays the art, culture and history of the American west. The staff displays Western culture and that of the indigenous peoples in unique and fascinating ways. Many have ranked its collection of Native American art as among the world's best. The museum staff collects Native American art and cultural object as well as artifacts from the old west. It is located on the Central Canal in White River State Park, White River State Park, downtown Indianapolis.

Eiteljorg Museum of American Indians & Western Art

500 W Washington St

Indianapolis, IN 46204

317-636-9378

https://www.eiteljorg.org/

Indiana History Center

Eugene and Marilyn Glick Indiana History Center

The Indiana Historical Society maintains changing exhibits throughout the year. These temporary exhibitions reflect the rich culture of the Hoosier State by showing photos, music, and other materials of Indiana history. In addition to the current exhibits, you may visit the William Henry Smith Memorial Library, the Basile History Market Gift Shop, Eli Lily Hall and the Cole Porter room. No admission is charged to visit the Indiana History Center.

Eugene and Marilyn Glick Indiana History Center

450 W. Ohio St.

Indianapolis, IN 46202

http://www.indianahistory.org/index.asp

White River State Park

White River State Park is located in downtown Indianapolis, Indiana and is adjacent to the Indianapolis Zoo. It is the state's only urban State Park, and one of the very few in the United States. From one facility, you can visit the Zoo, Botanical Gardens and Conservatory, and baseball game. It is within walking distance of the Indiana State Museum and IMAX Theatre.

Indianapolis Zoo

1200 W. Washington St.

Indianapolis, IN 46222

317-630-2001

info@indyzoo.com

http://www.indianapoliszoo.com/

Other Activities

During the summer months visitors to the canal may take a gondola ride, pilot a paddleboat, dine at one of the numerous or restaurants located on or near the canal. Located near the Indy Canal Walk, guest may also visit:

Medal of Honor Memorial

NCAA Museum

USS Indianapolis Memorial

For more information, contact:

Canal Walk

801 W. Washington St.

Indianapolis, IN 46204

317-233-2434

https://www.visitindy.com/indianapolis-canal-walk

Foellinger-Foellinger-Freimann Botanical Conservatory

Visitors to Fort Wayne must put a visit to the Foellinger-Foellinger-Freimann Botanical Conservatory at the top of their to-do list. The extensive conservatory and outdoor gardens provide several hours of enjoyment as you walk among the waterfalls and plants.

Brief History

Two friends, inspired by their visits to public gardens around the world, led an effort to open a world-class conservatory and botanical garden in Fort Wayne. Helene Foellinger and local attorney William V. Sowers worked diligently at their task. Their efforts paid off in 1983 with the opening of the Foellinger-Foellinger-Freimann Botanical Conservatory.

Helene Foellinger (December 12, 1910 - April 20, 1987)

The daughter of Oscar G. and Esther Anna (Deuter) Foelligner, Helene was native to Fort Wayne. After graduating from Fort Wayne's South Side High School, she attended the University of Illinois with an A.B. degree in mathematics. After graduating in 1932, she joined her father's newspaper, The Fort Wayne News-Sentinel, working as a reporter. Her father began grooming her to serve as president of the newspaper. Her father's death in 1936 vaulted her into the position of president when she was twenty-five. During the first five years of her tenure circulation increased dramatically. She would lead the newspaper for over forty years. She also became involved in several community organizations. She formed the Foellinger Foundation, through which she funneled funds for many community projects, including the Foellinger-Foellinger-Freimann Botanical Conservatory. Foellinger passed away in 1987 and is interred in Lindenwood Cemetery.

Short Indiana Road Trips

William V. Sowers (July 16, 1916 - September 15, 1993)

The son of Eugene Howard Sowers and Winnie Vance Sowers, was native to Winn parish, Louisiana. After serving as a Navy Reserve commander in World War II and the Korean war, Sowers worked as a lawyer in Indianapolis. He married Cornelia Sturgess Sowers. In 1949, he moved to Fort Wayne, Indiana where he joined the Fort Wayne National Bank. Sowers was heavily involved in community affairs and belonged to a number of organizations, including the Fort Wayne Park Foundation, the Allen County-Fort Wayne Historical Society and the Indiana chapter of the Nature Conservancy. He also served as a co-trustee of the Freimann Charitable Trust. Sowers passed away in 1993 and is interred in Lindenwood Cemetery in Fort Wayne.

In the Conservatory

Visitors to the 25,000 square feet conservatory will find a showcase, tropical and desert garden. The collection includes over 1,200 plants in more than 500 genera. The desert garden has over seventy-two different types of cacti.

The Outdoor Garden

Outdoors, visitors will find a Terrace, Exploration, Streetside and Beverforden Garden. The gardens include ornamental grasses, rhododendrons, trees, shrubs and perennials. The stunning displays of plants provide a wonderful gardening experience.

Gift and Plant Shop and Empyrean Café

Visitors can purchase plants grown at the conservatory as well as tasteful gifts from the Plant Shop. Lunch on tasty sandwiches, delectable deserts, or just have a light snack at the Empyrean Café.

Foellinger-Freimann Botanical Conservatory

1100 South Calhoun Street

Fort Wayne, IN 46802

(260) 427-6440

http://www.botanicalconservatory.org

Versailles State Park

Versailles State Park, located east of Versailles Indiana on US Route 50 is Indiana's second largest state park. It includes 5905 acres, the 230-acre Versailles Lake, a public swimming pool and one of the finest campgrounds in the Indiana State Park system. The northern area of the park features an extensive Mountain Bike trail system. Horse trails occupy the southern reaches. Wonderful hiking trails, fishing and boating are in between. Events at the park include the Bluegrass Festival the first weekend in October, a magnificent Fourth of July fireworks show and a Halloween even in late October.

Activities at Versailles State Park include:

Picnic Areas W/Shelters

Interpretive Naturalist Services (Seasonal)

Boat Launch Ramp

Boat Motor / Electric Trolling Only

Rental-Canoe, Paddleboat, Rowboat, and Kayak

Bridle Trails (Day Use Only)

Fishing

Hiking Trails

Mountain Bike Trails

Camping

Rental - Recreation Building

Swimming / Pool / Waterslide

Picnic Areas W/Shelters

The park has six picnic shelters, most of which nestle in secluded coves overlooking Versailles Lake. There are also additional picnic areas scattered throughout the park. Reserve shelters for family reunions, church dinners or other group activities at this link. http://www.indiana.reserveworld.com/

Interpretive Naturalist Services

A naturalist is available three days a week from Memorial Day to the middle of August. A seasonal interpretive naturalist offers hikes, educational and interpretive programs and evening activities. Program schedules available at this link (http://www.in.gov/dnr/parklake/2389.htm)or (812) 689-6424. Exhibits on park's natural and cultural history are on display at the Nature Center.

Rental-Canoe, Paddleboat, Rowboat, and Kayak

Paddleboats, kayaks and rowboats are available for rent at the marina. Visitors may use their own boats with trolling motors or oars on the lake.

Bridle Trails and Equine Day Use Facility (Day Use Only)

A horse day use area is located near Campground C. Equestrians may park their horse trailers here to load and unload their horses. A trail system for horses radiates out from the day use area that features twenty-five miles of trails. There is a tunnel passing under US 50, allowing access to the trails on the southern reaches of the park.

Fishing

Anglers may fish, with an Indiana State Fishing License, in the 230-acre Versailles Lake. Bank fish, use your own boat, or use a rental boat.

Camping

Electric / 226 sites

Group Camp

Youth Tent Camping Area

Dumping Station

The Class A campground has three sections with 226 electric sites only. There is no primitive camping. All sites accommodate tents or trailers and have electricity and fire rings. The campground has modern showers, restrooms, a playground and hot water. The campground is open year round. The restrooms, showers and other facilities close down from November until April. Winter camping rates apply during the winter months. Prospective visitors may reserve a campsite at this link.

Group Camping

Camp Laughery accommodates 120 persons. The complex includes sleeping cabins, kitchen, dining hall, shower house and a recreation hall. Camp Laughery is available from April through October, except for the recreation hall, which is open all year. Camp Laughery is near the Park Office. Reservations are available through the Central Reservation System.

Youth Tent Camping Area

The Youth Tent Camping Area includes three sites. Sites 1 and 2 will accommodate 25 tents each and Site 3 will house 35 tents. Each site has its own picnic shelter and fire ring and there is a pit toilet and water supply for the campground.

Camp Store

The camp store is located next to the Nature Center and swimming pool near the lake. Campers may purchase firewood and other supplies here.

Short Indiana Road Trips

Hiking Trails

Versailles State Park has about six miles of trails that make a wonderful hiking experience. The trails range from moderate to easy that traverse through impressive hardwood forests. Wildflowers blanket these forests in the spring.

Versailles State Park

Mailing Address:

P.O. Box 205

Versailles, IN 47042

(812) 689-6424

Mapping Address:

1004 U.S. 50

Versailles, IN 47042

http://www.in.gov/dnr/parklake/2963.htm

Visiting Nashville, Indiana

Little Nashville Indiana is located in the scenic hills of south central Indiana at the intersection of Indiana State Roads 46 and 135. It is about a mile west of Brown County State Park. Nashville is the county seat of Brown County.

While not a large town, Little Nashville is chuck full of shops, restaurants and coffee houses making it a delightful place to visit. Most of the buildings are patterned after early American architecture.

Shops

Most visitors come to Nashville to visit the small retail shops that dot the streets. These small stores offer a plethora of merchandise not found in the big box stores. Some of the offerings are locally made handcrafted merchandise. A local winery maintains a shop in the village, as well as numerous antique and art galleries, candle and gift stores. To find them all, you must peruse every little alleyway and street, as the stores are tucked in every conceivable corner. Resembling Gatlinburg, Tennessee, only smaller, Nashville maintains its own charm with an eclectic mix of art, antique and handicraft shops.

Restaurants

Diners in Nashville will find mostly small, locally owned establishments, which offer excellent food and atmosphere. Several bed and breakfasts in the village also have restaurants on the premises. Numerous coffee shops provide an opportunity for visitors to sip gourmet coffees and lattes.

Music and Theatre

Two theatres in Nashville, the Brown County Playhouse and the Melchior Marionette Theatre, provide venues for visitors to experience live, performance art in Nashville. The Bill Monroe's Bean Blossom Jamboree has live music and those wanting to shake a leg can do so at the Dance with Billy at the Dance Barn Monday Nights west of Nashville.

Art

Several artists, sculptors and other artisans maintain galleries in Nashville. The Brown County Art Guild displays works from fifty area artists. The nearby art studio of the late T. C. Steele provides a chance to look at the art and lifestyle of one of Indiana's leading artist. Steele laid the groundwork for today's arts community in the town.

Antiques

Shoppers will find an abundance of antique shops, flea markets and collectables stores while wandering Nashville's streets. Stores in nearby Bean Blossom and Gnaw Bone provide additional shopping opportunities.

Brown County Historical Museum Pioneer Village

Brown County Historical Museum consists of a two-story 1879 log jail, used until 1919. Visitors will also enjoy a two-story dogtrot log building, once used as a community building. It houses exhibits of Brown County schools and churches. Other displays include military items and a special exhibit of Cracker Jack memorabilia created by local artist Carey Cloud; an authentically restored log cabin with exhibits typical of the pioneer period; a working blacksmith shop circa 1850; an 1898 doctor's office used by Dr. Alfred J. Ralphy for nearly 50 years in Bellsville, in the southeastern part of the county. The newest addition to the Brown County Historical Museum Pioneer Village is a Woodworking Shop authentic to the 1850 period with the old tools and a shaving bench.

Brown County State Park

Visitors can explore the Brown County hills close up while hiking, camping or picnicking at nearby Brown County State Park. The Knobs terrain of southern Indiana provide almost

Appalachian style vistas from several overlooks in the park. Known as the "Little Smokies," no visit to Nashville is complete without a tour through Brown County State Park.

Lodging

Accommodations in Brown County range from camping at the state park to cabins, nifty cottages and comfortable bed and breakfasts.

Autumn in Brown County

Autumn in Brown County allows visitors to see the stunning fall foliage in Brown County. Visits in the fall can be busy, so make sure you make your reservations well ahead of time.

Nashville is one of Indiana's well-known gems. A road trip to Nashville will provide memories that will last a lifetime.

Brown County Convention & Visitors Bureau

P.O. Box 840

10 North Van Buren St.

Nashville, IN 47448

http://www.browncounty.com/

Short Indiana Road Trips

Anderson Falls

The Falls

Anderson Falls is a fourteen-foot waterfall that is almost one hundred feet wide on the Fall Fork of Clifty Creek. The falls formed because of a layer of Louisville Limestone overlying a less resilient layer of Waldron Shale. Visitors will see an impressive flow of water cascade over the falls, especially in the winter, spring and early summer when rainfall is abundant. The falls offers easy access as it is right along the road, adjacent to the parking area. A paved trail affords visitors a good view of it and a path down allows visitors to view the base.

Fall Fork Clifty Creek

The Fall Fork of Clifty Creek rises in Decatur County just west of Greensburg east of County Road 350 W and Indiana State Road 46 and south of Base Road. It flows through

Decatur County and into Bartholomew, finally entering Clifty Creek southwest of Hartsville.

Fall Fork of Clifty Creek in Bartholomew County

Length - About 3 miles

It flows into Bartholomew County from Decatur County between County Road 200 N and County Road 300 N after crossing County Road 1200 E. It crosses County Road 200 N twice before flowing northwest to its junction with Clifty Creek southwest of Hartsville and a little north of Indiana State Road 46.

Whitewater enthusiasts will find a whitewater rafting trail on this creek. The put in is at the western crossing of County Road 200 N. The take out spot is just above Anderson Falls. This is a 1.3-mile difficult run.

The Park

Purchased by the Nature Conservancy in 1977, the Bartholomew County Park Board now manages the forty-four acre Anderson Falls Nature Preserve. Thick forests surround the falls and a rich diversity of wildflowers populate the forest floor and canyon sides. The classic beech/maple forest also includes shagbark hickory, white oak and buckeye trees. The best time to visit for wildflowers is in the spring. Birdwatchers will delight in the abundant bird population that includes songbirds, hawks and woodpeckers. The park includes a picnic area, pit toilets and a nature trail.

Nature Trail

The trail network around the falls provides a wonderful hike. This area is actually the nature preserve and is open to the public. The moderate trail passes through the forest described earlier and in places offers a good view of the falls.

Short Indiana Road Trips

Note: the trail may be inaccessible, as hikers must cross the creek above or below the falls to access it.

Summer Wading

During the summer months, visitors to the falls may wade in the cool, rocky waters for some distance above the falls. On weekends, many locals visit the falls to cool off in the cascading waters.

Getting There

Visitors will find Anderson Falls about eight miles east of Columbus, Indiana on County Road 1140 E. To get to Anderson Falls, drive east from Columbus on Indiana State Road 46. About 1.35 miles from the SR 46 intersection with Indiana State Road 9 you will come to a little town called Newbern. About .6 miles from Newbern, you will want to turn right on County Road 925 E. After driving a very short distance, the road makes a ninety degree turn and becomes County Road 200 N. About 2.11 miles after this turn you will reach County Road 1140 E. Turn left. The parking lot is on the left, the falls is on the right.

For more information, contact:

Bartholomew County Park Board

Commissioner's Office

440 Third St

Columbus IN 47201.

http://www.bartholomew.in.gov/parks-and-recreation.html

Indiana Military Museum

Located in historic Vincennes, the Indiana Military Museum is home to one of the best, most comprehensive collections of military memorabilia in the country. The museum's collections contain weapons, uniforms, armor, aircraft and other military artifacts from all the wars and military actions in which the United States took part.

Inside the Museum

From the outside, the unimposing building displays no hint of the extent of the collection inside. Upon entering the museum, the signage and displays lead the visitor along an amazing tour of United States military history. An extensive array of photographs, charts, signs and weaponry allow the visitor to see the evolution of military weapons, uniforms and vehicles. The collection includes military paraphernalia from the following wars:

Revolutionary War

War of 1812

Mexican

Civil War

Spanish American War

World War I

World War II

Korean War

Vietnam War

Gulf War

The museum even includes a display of World War II items from Vincennes's favorite son, Red Skelton.

Short Indiana Road Trips

Outdoor Armor and Military Aircraft

Outdoors the visitor will find an extensive collection of military aircraft and armor. The collection includes Russian and Chinese military items as well as weaponry and vehicles from the United States Military. Visitors may walk inside a German D-Day style Bunker.

Museum Library

The Indiana Military Museum maintains an extensive military library, which visitors may use for research. Museum members may use the library as part of their membership dues; other visitors may use it as part of their admission fee.

Guided Museum Tours

Museum staff can give guided tours of the museum with advance notice.

Events

The museum hosts periodic displays of military items lent from other institutions. For a schedule of these events, call the museum or visit the web site.

For current hours, admission price and other notices, see the website.

Indiana Military Museum

715 South 6th Street

PO Box 977

Vincennes, IN 47591

Phone: (812) 882-1941

http://indianamilitarymuseum.org/

Model T Ford Museum

Visitors to Richmond may visit the Model T Ford Museum, maintained by the Model T Ford Club of America. The museum is the largest Model T club in the world that has models on display. The museum includes a gift shop rife with unique items.

The Model T Ford

Manufactured from October 1, 1908, to May 26, 1927, many regarded the Model T as the first affordable car for average people. The Ford Company utilized mass production techniques to build the car instead of the costly handcrafting car builders had previously used. The economical car had a tremendous impact on America and the world, spurring the demand for better roads, signage and maps. The Model T Changed American culture and along the way, it transformed the entire world.

Short Indiana Road Trips

Model T Ford Club of America

Organized in 1965, the Model T Ford Club of America has grown into the largest Model T club in the world. The club has over 100 chapters in the United States and several foreign countries. The club endeavors to preserve the history of the Model T Ford and its unique niche in American culture.

Model T Ford Museum

The museum is a delight to visit. The collection includes several functional Model T Ford cars, a 1925 fire truck, a 1927 coupe and a 1931 Pietenpol airplane powered by a Model T Engine.

Store

Visitors may browse the store, which is stocked with an extensive array of Model T apparel, books and other items. Much of the merchandise is also available for online sales on the web site.

Parts and Supplies

Model T owners may [purchase parts and supplies for their Model T online on the web site.

For more information on this wonderful museum, contact:

Model T Ford Museum

309 N. 8th Street

Richmond, IN 47374

(765) 488-0026

http://mtfca.com/

Indianapolis Artsgarden/Visitor Center

The Artsgarden is the centerpiece of downtown Indianapolis, spanning the busy Washington/Illinois intersection. It serves as the site for numerous events, concerts and art shows throughout the year. Visitors will also find a visitor center with many brochures, maps and books about Indianapolis and Marion County. A staffer on answers questions and provides information to curious tourists.

The Artsgarden

Designed by the New York architectural firm Ehrenkrantz Eckstut & Kuhn Architects, the 19,000 square foot Artsgarden spans the intersection of Washington and Illinois Streets. The Lily Endowment funded the twelve million dollar construction cost in 1995. Two 185-foot steel plate girders support the structure seventeen feet above the intersection. The top of the structure stands seven stories, or ninety-five feet above the floor of the Artsgarden. Over 32,000 square feet of glass covers the structure.

Ehrenkrantz Eckstut & Kuhn Architects

Founded in 1959 in Berkley, California by Ezra Ehrenkrantz as the Building Systems Development, the company underwent a series of mergers as it grew. Ehrenkrantz opened an office in New York in 1972, naming it the Ehrenkrantz Group. The company specializes in urban development, school and campus design and historic preservation, among other things. The company maintains offices in New York City, Washington DC, Los Angeles, and Shanghai, China.

Walkway

The Artsgarden serves primarily as a pedestrian walkway that allows people to travel, unimpeded by weather or traffic, across the busy Washington/Illinois Street intersection. It connects the downtown Circle Center Mall with hotels and other businesses on both sides of the street.

Events and Concerts

The Arts Council hosts over 250 events per year in the Artsgarden. These events range from free art exhibits to public concerts. The Artsgarden may also be rented for private parties, weddings and corporate events.

Fabulous Views of City

The 32,000 square feet of glass that enclose the structure afford some magnificent views of downtown Indianapolis down both Illinois and Washington Streets. Benches are provided for visitors to sit and watch traffic pass under them along both streets.

Weddings

It is possible to rent the Artsgarden for weddings. It has proven a popular nuptial venue. Rental fees from weddings and events support the various public arts programs that occur in the Artsgarden.

Arts Council of Indianapolis

The Arts Council of Indianapolis owns the Artsgarden and manages it. For more information about the Arts Council, contact:

Arts Council of Indianapolis

924 N. Pennsylvania St. (Mailing Address),

1 North Illinois (Physical Address of the Artsgarden)

Indianapolis, IN 46204

(317) 631-3301

indyarts@indyarts.org

https://indyarts.org

George Rogers Clark Home Site

The seven-acre tract that forms the George Rogers Home site is officially part of the Falls of the Ohio State Park. The site contains a reproduction of the cabin of General George Rogers Clark, a picnic area, boat ramp and historical markers. The site also has a reproduction of the cabin Clark's black servants, the McGee's lived in. Though humble, this spot sits high in American history, as it is the staging area for one of the greatest adventures of the United States of America, the Lewis and Clark Expedition.

General George Rogers Clark

Revolutionary War Hero General George Rogers Clark settled on this beautiful spot overlooking the grand Ohio River. General Clark's fame came from his exploits during the winter of 1778 during which he captured the three British posts in the Illinois country, Vincennes, Cahokia and Kaskaskia. This courageous expedition, composed of 175 men, took these posts without firing a shot, thus securing what would become the Northwest Territory from the British. Congress carved six states from this immense territory, Indiana, Illinois, Michigan, Wisconsin, Minnesota and Ohio. General Clark borrowed the money to fund the expedition. The United States Government never properly compensated him for his exploits and he spent most of his last days dealing with financial difficulties.

For his services, the State of Virginia awarded General Clark 150,000 acres, called the Clark Grant. This grant makes up most of current Clark County. Clark built a cabin and a gristmill on the spot occupied by the replica and lived there until 1809, when he had a stroke and fell into the fireplace, burning his leg. The leg needed amputation so he could no longer operate the mill. He moved to live with his brother-in-law in Kentucky, dying in 1818 after suffering another stroke.

Short Indiana Road Trips

General George Rogers Clark Cabin and His Servants the McGee's

The cabin on this spot is not the original cabin. There are no known drawings of that cabin, destroyed in 1854. This one comes from Ripley County, Indiana near the town of Osgood. The State of Indiana moved it here in 2001,

The smaller cabin is also a replica of the cabin occupied by Clark's servants, the McGee's. Technically slavery was illegal in the Northwest Territory so many slaves that lived there became free when the Northwest Ordinance became law. Many, lacking money to buy land, signed indentured servants agreements with their former masters. Their masters granted freedom and a tract of land to them as payment after a set period of servitude.

Interpretive Panels Describe the Gathering of the Corps of Discovery

William Clark, General Clark's younger brother, occupied the cabin with his brother. He kept up correspondence with President Thomas Jefferson, with whom both he and his brother George were friends. In 1803, he received a letter from the President requesting him to form up a company to explore the vast new acquisition, the Louisiana Territory that Jefferson had purchased from France in 1803. The cabin thus became a staging point for the Corps of Discovery. The expedition, now known as the Lewis and Clark Expedition, launched on the nearby river.

The Department of Natural Resources has erected several interpretative plaques outlining the beginnings of this voyage and the men that took part in the expedition.

Overlooking the Majestic Ohio River

Visitors, during the time the park is open, can browse through the cabins and meander through the grounds. There are picnic tables allowing the visitor to gaze out over the waters of the Ohio River as they enjoy their lunch.

Beginning the Lewis and Clark Expedition

The area is ripe with history as the final home of an American Revolutionary War hero, sometimes called the "Conqueror of the Northwest" General George Rogers Clark and his famous brother William Clark, one of the leaders of the Lewis and Clark Expedition.

George Rogers Clark Home Site

1102 W. Harrison Ave.

Clarksville, IN.

http://www.fallsoftheohio.org/clark_cabin.html

Short Indiana Road Trips

Lanier Mansion

The Lanier Mansion is an Indiana State Historic Site owned and managed by the Indiana State Museum. The 1834 mansion, built by James Lanier, is open for public tours and is well worth visiting.

History

Designed by architect Francis Costigan, the house was constructed between 1834 and 1835. During the time Lanier lived in the house, from 1844 until 1851, there were iron foundries to the north and east and hog lots to the east. The railroad station lay to the west and to the south Lanier had constructed the wharves and warehouses he needed to conduct business. The home features Corinthian columns, a spiral staircase, round doors and round, frieze windows.

State Ownership

The Lanier family owned the home until 1917, when the family donated it to Jefferson County. The State of Indiana acquired the house in 1925 to operate as a State Historic Site. The National Historic Landmark Foundation listed it on April 19, 1994.

James Lanier

James F.D. Lanier (November 22, 1800 – August 27, 1881)

Born in Washington, North Carolina to Alexander Chalmers and Drusilla Doughty Lanier, he migrated to Madison, Indiana at age 17 with his parents. He studied law at Transylvania University at Lexington, Kentucky, and then got a job as assistant clerk. He became the Clerk of the Indiana House of Representatives at Corydon. He assisted in the move when the capital transferred from Corydon to Indianapolis in 1825.

Finance

Lanier became involved in finance and became President of the Bank of Indiana, an institution he had helped the State of Indiana establish. He gained majority stocks in the Madison branch of that bank in 1833.

Railroads

By the late 1830's Lanier spearheaded the push to build the Madison and Indianapolis Railroad. This profitable railroad, along with his banking success, led to his accumulation of a large fortune. In 1844, he built his mansion in Madison, on a spot overlooking the Ohio River.

Financial Savior of Indiana

Lanier served twice to save the State of Indiana from financial ruin. In 1844, the State reeled from the massive Internal Improvement Act of 1836. The passage of the Act had strained the State's resources to the breaking point. He arranged with foreign investors to reduce the State's debt in return for transferring the property to the creditors. This saved the State from bankruptcy. During the Civil War, the Federal Government requested that Indiana raise and equip troops to fight in the war. Governor Oliver P. Morton requested that Lanier, who by now lived in New York, to lend the State a half million dollars. Lanier complied with the request and followed it up with a later loan of a half million dollars. He received no guarantee of repayment for these loans. The State did repay him by 1870.

To New York

Lanier moved to New York, never again to come to Indiana, in 1851 to manage new businesses he had started there. He died in 1881. The family retained possession of the mansion. His son, Alexander C. Lanier, lived in the home from 1851 until 1895, continuing to develop the home and garden during that time. The State of Indiana acquired the property and restored it. It is now a State Historic Site, open to the public.

Excerpted from the author's book:

Exploring Indiana's Historic Sites, Markers & Museums - South East Edition

http://indianaplaces.blogspot.com/2016/03/exploring-indianas-historic-sites_13.html

Francis Costigan

Native to Washington, DC, Costigan began his career in construction as a carpenter working in Baltimore. He studied architecture and became influenced by the work of New York architect Minard Lafever. An economic depression in Baltimore led him to migrate to the prosperous town of Madison, Indiana in 1837. During the time he spent in Madison, he developed an excellent reputation, designing many of the town's structure, including the old Madison

Hotel, the Shrewsbury home, Francis Costigan House as well as several others. Fourteen of his designs still stand in Madison's National Landmark Historic District. A brochure, available at Madison's Visitor Center, has a brochure that lists them. Costigan would migrate to Indianapolis in 1851, designing many of the buildings in the State Capital. These include the Institute for the Education of the Blind, the Bates House, and the Odd Fellows Building. Costigan died in Indianapolis and is interred at Crown Hill Cemetery.

Touring the Mansion

Visitors may tour the mansion. Museum staff conducts tours hourly, beginning on the hour. The tours visit all three levels of the home and allow some fine views of the river. Tickets are available at the Visitor Center at 601 First Street, which is just across from the mansion. Photos permitted, but no flash. The outside gardens are available to walk through at no charge.

For more information, contact:

Lanier Mansion

601 W. First Street

812-265-3526

Madison Indiana

https://www.indianamuseum.org/lanier-mansion-and-state-historic-site

VisitMadison, Inc.

601 W. First Street

Madison, IN 47250

http://www.visitmadison.org/

812-265-2956

Whitewater Canal State Historic Site

Whitewater Canal

Constructed as part of the Indiana Mammoth Internal Improvement Act of 1836 signed by Governor Noah Noble on January 27, 1836, the Whitewater Canal was to form an integral part of southeastern and eastern Indiana's transportation system. The ambitious act, in concert with the Panic of 1837, bankrupted the state and brought a major political party to its knees.

Indiana Mammoth Internal Improvement Act of 1836

The Internal Improvement Act was a too ambitious program of internal improvements that provided for the construction of canals and turnpikes. The ambitiousness of the program bankrupted the State of Indiana and caused the eventual demise and collapse of the Whig party, which favored the bill. The state assembly passed the bill that added ten million dollars to the state's budget at a time when its income was only about $65,000 annually.

Panic of 1837

This complex event created an economic depression that lasted from about 1837 until 1842. The multiple causes were questionable lending practices in the Western United States, restrictive lending policies enacted by Great Britain and falling agricultural prices. The period before 1837 had been a period of intense economic growth. During this time the prices of cotton and other commodities rose. Land prices also increased. The Bank of England noticed a decline in cash on hand in 1836. They raised interest rates in an attempt to attract more cash. When the Bank of England raised its interest, it forced banks in the United States and other nations to raise their rates. This, along with other events, caused land and cotton prices to fall. The chain of events this set off triggered a depression that caused profits, prices, and wages to fall and increased the unemployment rates. It was not until 1843 that the economies of the major countries rebounded.

Decline of the Whigs

The Whig party had pushed for the law and consequently bore the brunt of the blame. During the following years, the Whig Party collapsed, leaving the Democratic Party in control for many years.

Whitewater Canal

The Whitewater Canal's construction lasted from 1836 to 1847. During this time, there were many starts, pauses as the State of Indiana ran out of money, and the various private companies charged with completing also ran into financial difficulties. After completion, it connected Hagerstown, Indiana with Cincinnati, Ohio seventy-six miles to the south. The canal provided a quick, convenient way for farmers to transport their goods to market in the cities. Before the canal a farmer would need several days travel over deeply rutted roads to take his goods to Cincinnati. The canal proved a difficult construction project. It dropped 491 feet over the distance and needed fifty-six locks and seven dams. Several aqueducts to carry the canal over waterways also needed construction. Portions of the canal operated until 1862. The Whitewater Valley Railroad runs a part of the canal as a tourist attraction between Connersville and Metamora Indiana. The train runs alongside the canal and at Metamora visitors can ride a canal boat. The town of Metamora has many small shops and museums. The Indiana State Museum maintains an operating gristmill in the town as part of its network of Indiana State Historic Sites.

Short Indiana Road Trips

The Gristmill

Build by Jonathan Banes in 1845, the mill has used the current of the Whitewater Canal as a power source ever since.

Brief History by the Author

Jonathan Banes (February 12, 1817 - April 13, 1906)

The son of Jonathan and Anna (Gillingham) Banes, Jonathan was native to Buck's County, Pennsylvania. He apprenticed to a carpenter in Montgomery County, Pennsylvania after leaving home at age sixteen. After completing his apprenticeship, he worked in Philadelphia for a time, and then migrated to Brookville in 1837 when he heard the news of the construction of the Whitewater Canal. He gained employment doing construction on the canal project, becoming the supervisor of many of the structures on the canal. These projects included the Brookville dam, several of the locks and bridges on the canal. Banes Married Maria Mount, the daughter of Judge David Mount, on September 5, 1841. The couple would have two sons, William Mount and Mary. The state suspended work on the canal in the fall of 1839. Banes did not receive payment until spring, 1840. He took the funds, purchased some horses and drove them to Pennsylvania to sell. After completing the sale, he returned to Brookville. He moved to Metamora open the Metamora Cotton Factory in 1845. He built his home in Metamora the same year he built the mill. The house, the Banes Home, houses a gift shop and the "Banes Suite for Two," which visitors may rent during a stay in Metamora. Banes would convert the cotton mill to a gristmill in 1856. After selling the mill, Banes became a farmer and land investor. He is interred with his wife in Metamora Cemetery, Metamora.

Metamora Cotton Factory

Equipped with 1000 spindles to spin raw cotton into thread, the three-story mill opened in 1845. Bane had to import the cotton from the south because it is not grown in Indiana. The canal made it less expensive to import cotton cloth and ready-made clothing, thus the mill became unprofitable. Bane removed the cotton making machinery and installed equipment to grind grains into flour and meal. Several cotton mills operated in the state of Indiana during this period, using the power of water to spin raw cotton or wool into thread. Known variously as the Hoosier Mills and Crescent Mill, a fire destroyed the building in 1899. The mill was rebuilt, but fire destroyed that building in 1932. The current two-story building was built the same year.

State Historic Site

The Indiana State Museum currently operates the mill, grinding corn into meal that visitors may purchase as they watch the waterwheel use the canal's energy to turn the immense grist wheels. Visitors to the mill may also purchase tickets to ride the canal boat, the Ben Franklin. For information on hours and events, contact:

Whitewater Canal State Historic Site

19083 Clayborne St.

Metamora, In 47030,

765-647-6512

http://www.indianamuseum.org/whitewater-canal-state-historic-site

Whitewater Canal State Historic Site

Open from April through November, the Whitewater Canal State Historic Site is free. Visitors may purchase mill products inside the gristmill, watch the mill wheel turn or ride the canal boat, Ben Franklin. Special rates are available for schoolchildren. Groups may rent the facility for special occasions. Check the web site or call the phone number listed below for events, hours, admission prices and other information.

Whitewater Canal State Historic Site

19083 Clayborne St.

Metamora, In 47030, Usa

765-647-6512

whitewatercanalshs@indianamuseum.org

http://www.indianamuseum.org/whitewater-canal-state-historic-site

Whitewater Valley Railroad

The demise of the Whitewater Canal planted the seeds for the Whitewater Valley Railroad in the mid 1850's when floods washed out large portions of the canals. Franklin County residents petitioned the State of Indiana, asking that the state sell the canal towpath route to use as a railroad. In 1863 the Indianapolis and Cincinnati Railroad purchased the rights to the towpath and built a line from Brookville to Hagerstown, Indiana. Portions of the canal remained open and became useful as power sources for gristmills like the one at Metamora. The Whitewater Canal remained open in Metamora until 1953. Western Avenue now covers it.

The First Whitewater Valley Railroad

The first Whitewater Valley Railroad was a subsidiary of the Indianapolis and Cincinnati Railroad. This subsidiary began construction of the rail line from Brookville, reaching Connersville in 1867. The line punched through to Hagerstown the next year. The Big Four, Cleveland, Cincinnati, Chicago & St. Louis, Railroad purchased the

Indianapolis and Cincinnati Railroad in 1890. This line became the New York Central in later years. These lines operated both freight and passenger trains. The line discontinued passenger service in 1933. Freight service ground to a halt in the late 1970's and early 1980's.

The Second Whitewater Valley Railroad

Formed as a non-profit organization in 1972, the Whitewater Valley Railroad operates as a operating railroad museum. The all volunteer staff runs both historic diesel and steam engines on the eighteen mile line between Connersville and Metamora. For more information about train schedules, the history and other information, contact:

Whitewater Valley Railroad

455 Market St,

Connersville, IN 47331

(765) 825-2054

http://www.whitewatervalleyrr.org

Short Indiana Road Trips

About the Author

Paul considers himself a bit of an Indiana hound, in that he likes to sniff out the interesting places and history of Indiana and use his books to tell people about them.

Join Paul on Facebook

https://www.facebook.com/Mossy-Feet-Books-474924602565571/

Twitter

https://twitter.com/MossyFeetBooks

mossyfeetbooks@gmail.com

Mossy Feet Books Catalog

To Get Your Free Copy of the Mossy Feet Books Catalogue, Click This Link.

http://mossyfeetbooks.blogspot.com/

Gardening Books

Fantasy Books

Humor

Science Fiction

Semi – Autobiographical Books

Travel Books

Short Indiana Road Trips

Sample –

Driving the Canals and Rivers Auto Trail

Franklin County Historical Marker - Metamora Grist Mill

Inscription

In 1845, Jonathan Banes built a three-story frame cotton mill, known as Metamora Cotton Factory, on this site. Banes, a former contractor on the canal, converted the cotton factory to a flouring mill in 1856, and sold the mill to John Curry in 1857.

Over the next several years, the mill was operated by various owners and was known first as Hoosier Mills and later as Crescent Mills. The original mill was destroyed by a fire in 1899 and was rebuilt in 1900. Following a second fire in 1932, it was converted to the present two-story brick building.

Purchased by the State of Indiana

In 1946, the State of Indiana purchased a 14-mile section of the Whitewater Canal, including the mill, as a state historic site. Today the mill grinds both white and yellow corn into corn meal and grits, and wheat into whole-wheat flour and cereal. The millstones are powered by the 12-foot breast water wheel in the canal behind the mill.

Brief History by the Author

Jonathan Banes (February 12, 1817 - April 13, 1906)

The son of Jonathan and Anna (Gillingham) Banes, Jonathan was native to Buck's County, Pennsylvania. He apprenticed to a carpenter in Montgomery County, Pennsylvania after leaving home at age sixteen. After completing his apprenticeship, he worked in Philadelphia for a time, then migrated to Brookville in 1837 when he heard the news of the construction of the Whitewater Canal. He gained employment doing construction on the canal project, becoming the supervisor of many of the structures on the canal. These projects included the Brookville dam, several of the locks and bridges on the canal. Banes Married Maria Mount Banes, the daughter of Judge David Mount, on September 5, 1841. The couple would have two sons, William Mount and Mary. The state suspended work on the canal in the fall of 1839. Banes did not receive payment until spring, 1840. He took the funds, purchased some horses and drove them to Pennsylvania to sell. After completing the sale, he returned to Brookville. He moved to Metamora open the Metamora Cotton Factory in 1845. He built his home in Metamora the same year he built the mill. The house, the Banes Home, houses a gift shop and the "Banes Suite for Two," which visitors may rent during a stay in Metamora. Banes would convert the cotton mill to a gristmill in 1856. After selling the mill, Banes became a farmer and land investor. He is interred with his wife in Metamora Cemetery, Metamora.

Metamora Cotton Factory

Equipped with 1000 spindles to spin raw cotton into thread, the three-story mill opened in 1845. Bane had to import the cotton from the south because it is not grown in Indiana. The canal made it less expensive to import cotton cloth and ready-made clothing, thus the mill became unprofitable. Bane removed the cotton making machinery and installed equipment to grind grains into flour and meal. Several cotton mills operated in the state of Indiana during this period, using the power of water to spin raw cotton or wool into thread.

State Historic Site

The Indiana State Museum currently operates the mill, grinding corn into meal that visitors may purchase as they watch the waterwheel use the canal's energy to turn the immense grist wheels. Visitors to the mill may also purchase tickets to ride the canal boat, the Ben Franklin.

Whitewater Canal State Historic Site

19083 Clayborne St.

Metamora, In 47030, USA

765-647-6512

http://www.indianamuseum.org/whitewater-canal-state-historic-site

Mossy Feet Books

www.mossyfeetbooks.com

Made in the USA
Monee, IL
17 February 2023